T0286821

Renewing U.S. Security Policy in the Middle East

SHELLY CULBERTSON, HOWARD J. SHATZ, STEPHANIE STEWART

Prepared for Office of the Secretary of Defense
Approved for public release; distribution unlimited

NATIONAL DEFENSE RESEARCH INSTITUTE

For more information on this publication, visit **www.rand.org/t/RRA904-1**.

About RAND

The RAND Corporation is a research organization that develops solutions to public policy challenges to help make communities throughout the world safer and more secure, healthier and more prosperous. RAND is nonprofit, nonpartisan, and committed to the public interest. To learn more about RAND, visit www.rand.org.

Research Integrity

Our mission to help improve policy and decisionmaking through research and analysis is enabled through our core values of quality and objectivity and our unwavering commitment to the highest level of integrity and ethical behavior. To help ensure our research and analysis are rigorous, objective, and nonpartisan, we subject our research publications to a robust and exacting quality-assurance process; avoid both the appearance and reality of financial and other conflicts of interest through staff training, project screening, and a policy of mandatory disclosure; and pursue transparency in our research engagements through our commitment to the open publication of our research findings and recommendations, disclosure of the source of funding of published research, and policies to ensure intellectual independence. For more information, visit www.rand.org/about/principles.

RAND's publications do not necessarily reflect the opinions of its research clients and sponsors.

Published by the RAND Corporation, Santa Monica, Calif.
© 2022 RAND Corporation
RAND® is a registered trademark.

Library of Congress Cataloging-in-Publication Data is available for this publication.
ISBN: 978-1-9774-0722-1

Cover image composite: Design, D. Carol Ponce, Pasko Maksim/Adobe Stock

About This Report

Changing political, security, and economic contexts in the United States and the Middle East call for improved U.S. approaches to managing its interests in the Middle East. This report offers a new framing of U.S. security interests in the region and provides recommendations for addressing these interests. This report will be of interest to U.S. government officials with responsibilities related to national security and the Middle East, policymakers in the Middle East, scholars of the Middle East, and others focusing on the region. This research was completed in September 2021, before the October 2021 U.S. withdrawal from Afghanistan, the February 2022 Russian invasion of Ukraine, and the 2021–2022 suspension of certain democratic processes in Tunisia. It has not been subsequently revised.

This research was sponsored by the Office of the Secretary of Defense and conducted within the International Security and Defense Policy Center of the RAND National Security Research Division (NSRD), which operates the RAND National Defense Research Institute (NDRI), a federally funded research and development center (FFRDC) sponsored by the Office of the Secretary of Defense, the Joint Staff, the Unified Combatant Commands, the Navy, the Marine Corps, the defense agencies, and the defense intelligence enterprise.

For more information on the International Security and Defense Policy Center, see www.rand.org/nsrd/isdp or contact the director (contact information is provided on the webpage).

Contents

Tables

Summary

This report offers a new framing of U.S. national security interests in the Middle East in light of the changed political, security, and economic contexts in the region; the new U.S. administration and mounting global challenges; a greater U.S. security focus on China and Russia; and the coronavirus 2019 (COVID-19) pandemic.[1] It lays out the range of U.S. security interests there, some of which are traditional and some of which are not typically considered, and provides recommendations on how to achieve the goals these interests reflect. If not managed proactively, these issues will continue to draw the United States into reactive military engagements, as has happened repeatedly in recent decades. Therefore, new approaches from the United States are called for.

Although there have been loud calls for the United States to deprioritize the Middle East and retrench from it militarily, the region sits at the crossroads of multiple vital U.S. interests. Problems that start in the Middle East spread worldwide. This report makes the case that the United States should not deprioritize or disengage from the Middle East. Instead, even as it reduces military presence in the region to free resources for competition with Russia and China, it should recognize the full range of its interests and manage these in a proactive, consistent, and integrated way that relies less on military operations as primary tools; increases use of the United States' other considerable sources of power, including diplomatic, economic, and technical assistance tools; and safeguards U.S. interests over the long term.

This report drew on an extensive literature review, consultation with RAND experts about various topics, and author expertise.

---

[1] This research was completed in September 2021, before the October 2021 U.S. withdrawal from Afghanistan, the February 2022 Russian invasion of Ukraine, and the 2021–2022 suspension of certain democratic processes in Tunisia. It has not been subsequently revised.

The Changing Context in Both the United States and the Middle East Means New U.S. Security Approaches Are Required

Any new approach toward the Middle East will need to account for significant changes in context in both the United States and the Middle East.

The Biden administration's priorities are of necessity managing problems at home—addressing public health needs related to the COVID-19 pandemic and helping the American economy recover. U.S. foreign and security policy is also increasingly emphasizing great power competition. Furthermore, any new approach should also recognize that the United States has proven time and again that it cannot simply leave the Middle East. In recent decades, the United States has engaged in a reactive cycle of attempting to disengage from the Middle East, followed by new military engagement. Indeed, every administration since that of Jimmy Carter has initiated new military action in the region in response to events that threaten American strategic interests, such as those related to terrorism, energy, or attacks on American forces. These actions have been of different scales, ranging from major wars to more targeted military activities. Such an approach has led to chasing symptoms, not proactively managing underlying problems, and therefore to incoherent policy that fails to meet objectives.

The Middle East security landscape is also very different now than it has been in recent decades. This means that U.S. national security interests in the region, and the risks posed to these interests, have evolved in ways that call for a modified set of priorities. Some of the key changes are as follows. For the first time in nearly two decades since 9/11, the United States is not involved in major wartime operations in the greater Middle East. Ten years after the 2011 Arab Spring, while there have been few tangible improvements, the movement's aspirations still shape actions of citizens and governments. There are many festering conflicts, such as in Syria, Yemen, and Libya, as well as the ongoing Israeli-Palestinian conflict. Despite some early momentum in conflict resolution, prospects for near-term resolution are dim. Although it remains important, the Israeli-Palestinian conflict is no longer the single epicenter of Middle East tensions, as there are multiple other heated conflicts, and the Abraham Accords normalized relations between more Arab countries and Israel. The health and economic pressures of the pandemic will not let up in the Middle East, where vaccine roll-out could take several years. Relations with Iran are much worse, with new discussions but no agreement to pause nuclear and other malign activities. The Middle East is now a theater for great power competition with China and Russia. Yet there have also been important successes, such as the defeat of the Islamic State in Iraq and Syria (ISIS), the Abraham Accords, and improving public services in some countries.

A Top-Ten List of U.S. Security Interests in the Middle East

Three issues have dominated U.S. security efforts in recent decades: preventing terrorism, protecting global energy markets, and dealing with Iranian nuclear proliferation and other malign activities. This report makes the case that in addition to these, the United States now has an even wider set of security interests in the region, some of which have not historically been considered security interests but are. We present a top-ten list of the U.S. security issues in the Middle East that require ongoing, integrated U.S. engagement.

Terrorist groups are degraded, but they still have capabilities. Many of the underlying conditions that lead to support for violent extremism in the Middle East still exist or are worse. Military means alone will not be sufficient to address this issue, which require diplomacy and improvement of governance and economic conditions.

While the United States now relies less on Middle East energy, its allies still depend on it. The United States has served as a guarantor of the stability of global energy markets since shortly after World War II. A reduced American role would leave a vacuum that could strengthen the leverage of Russia and China over U.S. European and Asian allies. U.S. military forces are not necessarily needed to safeguard supply, but a U.S. backup can be useful to support regional navies.

The Middle East is a hot spot for nuclear proliferation threats. U.S. nonproliferation efforts there focus mainly on Iran: Should Iran gain nuclear weapons, Saudi Arabia or Turkey could follow. Any Iran nuclear policy will need to consider containment of Iran's ballistic missile programs, sponsorship of proxy forces, and treatment of U.S. regional allies as well.

The Middle East is a theater for great power competition. Great power competition with China and Russia remains the centerpiece of U.S. security policy, and the Middle East will remain important to this competition. Even if neither China nor Russia is trying to supplant the United States there, both have objectives there that counter U.S. interests. China's main interests are economic, as it has become a top regional trading partner and investor. Russia engages diplomatically and militarily. In selling weapons to U.S. adversaries—such as Iran—Russia can help fuel destabilizing conflicts, and in selling to U.S. partners and allies—such as Turkey and Egypt—Russia can strain strategic relationships. Nonetheless, there are areas in which Russia, China, and the United States share interests.

Regional conflicts and aggression strain world order and affect U.S. security. Multiple civil wars and conflicts spill over, as battle-trained terrorists move across countries, resulting weak states provide vacuums that create space for proxy wars, and conflicts create destabilizing refugee flows. Resolving conflicts is a core interest of the United States in the region.

Militarized approaches have had high human and financial costs. Nearly all American military deaths in the past four decades have been in the Middle East, and veterans face physical and mental health problems. One estimate is that the United States has spent $6.4 trillion on wars in Iraq, Syria, Afghanistan, and Pakistan. Comparatively, spending on foreign assistance and security cooperation in the Middle East is paltry.

Civilian displacement is harmful and destabilizing. The Middle East has a greater proportion of its population displaced by violence than any other region of the world. There is no plan underway for solutions. This may create space for future radicalization. Migration flows out of the Middle East have been a destabilizing factor for the European Union.

Climate change impacts exacerbate other security challenges. The Middle East is the hottest and most water-poor region in the world. Climate change may undermine regional security through the loss of livelihood from loss of arable land, state competition over water resources, or effects on mass migration. At the same time, a focus on climate change through a security lens offers some opportunities to find common ground in regional negotiations.

The United States benefits from the well-being of its allies and partners. The region has one North Atlantic Treaty Organization (NATO) ally, seven formally designated U.S. Major Non-NATO Allies, and two "major security partners." The U.S. military has some kind of military presence in at least 12 countries in the region. U.S. credibility as an alliance partner is a factor in the extent to which allies will support U.S. goals, and it is in U.S. interests to maintain these strong relations.

Weak rule of law and economic opportunities lead to chronic instability that spills over to the rest of the world. Protests and government overthrows in 2011 and 2018–2021 reflect frustration over two main issues: lack of economic opportunity and problems of governance—in particular, corruption. Overall, these conditions are not improving. Insofar as turmoil in the Middle East has consistently spilled over into security threats for the United States, we believe that American security interests in the Middle East are inherently tied to improved economic opportunities and more accountable governance.

Recommendations

The Middle East is central to many issues that affect American national security. We present recommendations to manage these interests by reducing reliance on military tools and increasing reliance on civilian tools. Some of these recommendations are new because of the changed context while others may be newly possible because of these changes. At the same time, each of these recommendations has risks, constraints, and trade-offs, and not all can be done at once.

Develop a U.S. interagency Middle East strategy that keeps the region as a priority while relying more on civilian tools. The U.S. government should develop and publicly articulate an interagency strategy for the Middle East that defines U.S. interests and goals, integrates and rebalances military tools with other tools, and increases reliance on civilian agencies in order to focus activities and explain to the America public the U.S. strategy.

Develop substitute approaches to manage risks when reducing the U.S. military footprint in the Middle East. In the context of a U.S. global force posture review underway in 2021 with a mandate to shift resources to Asia, reductions in the U.S. military footprint should include substitute approaches to manage risks, in line with the recommended strategy above. Other experts have noted multiple options such as rotations; offloading responsibilities to regional partners; regional ballistic missile defenses; new approaches to intelligence, surveillance, and reconnaissance; maintaining the most strategic presence; and increasing security cooperation with nations in the Middle East

Maintain an integrated, long-term strategy with regard to Iran. The United States should keep the full set of strategic interests in mind in dealing with Iran: nuclear nonproliferation, ballistic missiles, sponsorship of proxy militias, attacks on U.S. bases and troops, cyberattacks, stoking of sectarian tensions, ongoing destabilizing competition with Saudi Arabia, and competition for influence with the United States in Iraq. A containment and de-escalation approach could manage risks while checking Iran's most threatening activities. The United States should ensure that its force posture and security cooperation are sufficient to support allies in containing Iran.

Mediate the end of conflicts, and broker pragmatic solutions to civilian displacement. As the United States played successful roles in defeating ISIS and facilitating the Abraham Accords, a next priority for the United States should be leading diplomatic efforts to resolve other conflicts and finding solutions for all refugees and internally displaced persons (IDPs) in the Middle East in the next ten years.

Focus U.S. development assistance on addressing the two main causes of the Arab Spring protests. The Arab Spring and Arab Spring 2.0 protests have led to instability and created security challenges for the United States and its allies. It is in U.S. security interests to help overcome these challenges. The United States should focus its development assistance on addressing two key drivers of Arab Spring protests and their aftermath: the lack of economic opportunities for youth and problems of corruption within governments, and with police in particular.

Improve trust in the United States as a strong, effective, reliable partner of choice. The positive opinion of the United States in the Middle East has declined. Meeting security goals in the Middle East depends on the quality of relationships, as well as regard for U.S. capability to take leadership to solve vexing problems.

Maintain an integrated program for countering violent extremism. The United States should implement an interagency strategy that uses both military and civilian tools, develop a better understanding of deradicalization apart from military interventions, continue targeted efforts against extremist groups, support regional government efforts in doing so through capacity-building of law enforcement and other agencies, and find solutions for detained ISIS families.

Facilitate regional interactions, mutual assistance, and security dialogues. The Middle East is the only region without a functioning forum for security dialogue and cooperation on issues of importance. Both the Barack Obama and Donald Trump administrations supported the proposed Middle East Strategic Alliance, which aims to integrate military, energy, political, and economic security and problem-solving. The Biden administration should revive discussions.

Invest in encouraging the linchpin countries of Iraq and Tunisia on the path to success. These two countries in the Middle East merit a special push for U.S. technical assistance in security, in economic reforms, and in judicial and justice procedures. Iraq is a U.S. strategic partner, is recovering from war with ISIS, and is a theater for U.S. competition with Iran. Tunisia is the only country, after overthrowing its government during the Arab Spring, to embark on the kinds of initiatives that address the causes of the protests. However, Tunisia's economy remains stagnant and is not providing adequate jobs for its youth. The Middle East needs examples of countries that have addressed these problems successfully.

Acknowledgments

The authors thank their RAND colleagues Colin Clarke, Ben Connable, Louay Constant, Dalia Dassa Kaye, James Dobbins, Daniel Egel, Susan Everingham, Carrie Farmer, Todd Helmus, Krishna Kumar, Jennifer Moroney, David Ochmanek, Miranda Priebe, Linda Robinson, and David Thaler for invaluable discussions that contributed to this essay. They also thank Agnes Schaefer and Laura Baldwin for their support in enabling this project, Nathan Vest for contributing to the literature review, and Stephanie Lonsinger for her work on the references. Reviews by Jon Alterman and Jeffrey Martini strengthened the report considerably. All errors of fact and interpretation remain the responsibility of the authors.

Abbreviations

COVID-19	Coronavirus 2019
DoD	Department of Defense
EIA	U.S. Energy Information Administration
FY	fiscal year
IDP	internally displaced person
ISIS	Islamic State in Iraq and Syria
ISR	intelligence, surveillance, and reconnaissance
JCPOA	Joint Comprehensive Plan of Action
MENA	Middle East and North Africa
MESA	Middle East Strategic Alliance
NATO	North Atlantic Treaty Organization
OEF	Operation Enduring Freedom
OIF	Operation Iraqi Freedom
UNHCR	United Nations High Commissioner for Refugees
USAID	U.S. Agency for International Development

CHAPTER 1

Introduction

A new administration and mounting global challenges provide an opportunity to take critical stock of U.S. interests, investments, and policy tools in the Middle East and choose the ones that best meet U.S. objectives. Some have called for deprioritization of the Middle East in comparison with other regions, a retrenchment from it, or a reduction in American engagement there. This reflects several issues: (1) frustration among policymakers with long-lasting wars and perceptions of poor results in meeting U.S. goals after decades of investment in the Middle East; (2) a shift to focusing security assets on great power competition with China and Russia per the 2018 National Defense Strategy and more distinctly on China with the 2021 Interim National Security Strategic Guidance, along with a renewed effort to strengthen alliances to better conduct great power competition,[1] and (3) a perception of the declining importance of the Middle East to U.S. security interests in comparison with the past.[2] For instance, Mara Karlin and Tamara Cofman Wittes wrote in an oft-

---

[1] This research was completed in September 2021, before the October 2021 U.S. withdrawal from Afghanistan, the February 2022 Russian invasion of Ukraine, and the 2021–2022 suspension of certain democratic processes in Tunisia. It has not been subsequently revised.

[2] Andrew J. Bacevich, *America's War for the Greater Middle East: A Military History*, New York: Random House, 2016; The White House, *Interim National Security Strategic Guidance*, Washington, D.C., March 2021c; Robert A. Manning and Peter A. Wilson, "Offshore Balancing Approach Can Correct America's Middle East Approach," *The National Interest*, February 26, 2021; and U.S. Department of Defense (DoD), *Summary of the 2018 National Defense Strategy of the United States of America: Sharpening the American Military's Competitive Edge*, Washington, D.C., 2018.

cited *Foreign Affairs* piece that the Middle East "matters markedly less than it used to."[3] Martin Indyk wrote in a *Wall Street Journal* commentary entitled "The Middle East Isn't Worth It Anymore" that "few vital interests of the U.S. continue to be at stake in the Middle East."[4]

However, the Middle East sits at the crossroads of multiple vital U.S. interests, and problems that start there spread worldwide.[5] The United States has a wider range of security interests there than are typically considered. If not managed properly, Middle East issues will continue to draw the United States into reactive military engagements as has happened repeatedly in recent decades. These security interests instead require careful management in a strategic, long-term, and consistent way.

This report makes the case that not only do the three historic U.S. security interests in the Middle East remain—namely, countering terrorism, protecting energy markets, and ensuring nuclear nonproliferation—but that the United States now has an even wider set of security interests in the region, some of which have not traditionally been considered security interests. Therefore, the United States should not deprioritize or disengage from the Middle East. Instead, even as it reduces military presence in the region to free resources for competition with Russia and China, it should recognize the full range of its interests there and manage these in a proactive, consistent, integrated, and long-term way that relies less on military operations as primary tools and increases reliance on the United States' other considerable sources of power. We offer a new framing of U.S. national security interests in the Middle East in light of the changed political, security, and economic context in the Middle East; the new U.S. administration; greater U.S. secu-

---

[3] Mara Karlin and Tamara Cofman Wittes, "America's Middle East Purgatory: The Case for Doing Less," *Foreign Affairs*, January/February 2019.

[4] Martin Indyk, "The Middle East Isn't Worth It Anymore," *Wall Street Journal*, January 17, 2020.

[5] The region is a literal crossroads of importance to the United States and its allies as well, with the Suez Canal serving as the main artery for ocean shipping between Europe and Asia (Theo Notteboom, Athanasios Pallis, and Jean-Paul Rodrigue, "Main Routing Alternatives Between East Asia and Northern Europe," *Port Economics, Management and Policy*, 2021).

rity challenges stemming from Asia; and circumstances of the coronavirus 2019 (COVID-19) pandemic.

A Changing Context in the United States Requires New U.S. Security Approaches Toward the Middle East

Any new approach toward the Middle East will need to account for three significant changes in context in the United States.

First, the Biden administration's priorities are of necessity managing problems at home—addressing public health needs related to the pandemic and helping the American economy recover. The domestic expenditures by the federal government associated with the pandemic have made it clear that activities outside of the United States need to be much more cost efficient, and choices must be made about priorities in order to cut costs while not neglecting security interests.

Second, U.S. foreign and security policy is increasingly emphasizing great power competition with Russia and China, although with a greater focus on China. Indeed, the Biden administration's 2021 Interim National Security Strategic Guidance states the need to prioritize the defense budget to free up resources for maintaining national security advantages over China and Russia and orders a review of the U.S. global force posture, which includes guidance to "right-size" military presence in the Middle East to deter terrorism and Iranian aggression and protect other interests.[6] It also began steps to trim U.S. military capabilities and forces in the Gulf.[7]

Third, United States policy toward the Middle East itself has not fully taken into account the dramatic changes that have taken place in there, as discussed more fully in the next section. These changes mean that the United States needs a strategy for the Middle East that assesses and takes

---

[6] The White House, March 2021c.

[7] Gordon Lubold and Warren P. Strobel, "Biden Trimming Forces Sent to Mideast to Help Saudi Arabia," *Wall Street Journal*, April 2, 2021.

account of the changed context; defines security interests; articulates goals; and makes better use of its full range of military, diplomatic, economic, and other tools.

Furthermore, most Americans continue to view the Middle East as important, despite frustration with long-lasting wars and violence in the region. A 2020 Chicago Council on Global Affairs survey found that a bipartisan majority (61 percent) of Americans viewed the Middle East as the most important region to U.S. national security interests due to threats from terrorism and Iran's activities; this was up from half of those surveyed in 2018.[8] Three-quarters of those surveyed in 2020 supported maintaining or increasing the U.S. troop presence. Gallup polls find that Americans view particular issues in the Middle East as threats to the vital interests of the United States. More than 95 percent of Americans viewed international terrorism and development of nuclear weapons by Iran as critical or important threats, and more than 85 percent viewed the conflict in Syria and the conflict between Israel and the Palestinians as critical or important. More than 75 percent identified as vitally important or important to the United States what happens in particular Middle East countries: Egypt, Iran, Iraq, Israel, and Syria.[9]

Any new approach should recognize that the United States has proven time and again that it cannot simply leave the Middle East because of enduring security interests. Indeed, dating back to the beginning of the United States as a country, the U.S. Navy was founded to confront threats from the Barbary pirates, based in what is now Morocco, Tunisia, Algeria, and Libya, who were attacking U.S. merchant ships.[10] In recent decades, the United States has engaged in a reactive cycle of attempting to disengage from the Middle East, then confronting a threat, followed by military engagement or reactive diplomacy, followed by withdrawal, followed by new military engagement. This cycle was most recently illustrated by the U.S. invasion of Iraq in 2003, which was followed by an Iraqi insurgency, then a U.S. military

---

[8] Dina Smeltz and Craig Kafura, *American Public Support for U.S. Troops in Middle East Has Grown*, Chicago, Ill.: The Chicago Council on Global Affairs, February 10, 2020.

[9] Gallup, "U.S. Position in the World," Gallup, 2021.

[10] Office of the Historian, Foreign Service Institute, "Barbary Wars, 1801–1805 and 1815–1816," webpage, undated b; Michael B. Oren, *Power, Faith, and Fantasy: America in the Middle East, 1776 to the Present*, New York: W.W. Norton, 2011.

surge in 2008 to counter the surge, then U.S. withdrawal in 2011, then the rise of the Islamic State in Iraq and Syria (ISIS) in Iraq in 2014, which was enabled by the vacuum created when the United States pulled out, then the United States engaging again in 2014 to defeat ISIS.

Such an approach has led to chasing symptoms, not proactively solving let alone managing underlying problems. This pattern has led to incoherent policy that fails to meet objectives.[11] It also shows that the United States becomes complacent about managing its security interests in the Middle East at its peril—in particular if it wishes to avoid the reactive cycle undertaken in recent years.

Indeed, most new administrations have begun either with aspirations of reduced military activity in the Middle East or at least without plans for increased military engagement. Despite this, the Middle East repeatedly pulls the United States in. Every administration since that of President Jimmy Carter has initiated new military action in the Middle East in reaction to events that threaten American strategic interests, such as those related to terrorism, energy, or attacks on American forces. These actions have been of different scales, with the administrations of George H. W. Bush, George W. Bush, and Barack Obama engaging in major wars; the administration of Donald Trump finishing an ongoing major war; and the administrations of Jimmy Carter, Ronald Reagan, Bill Clinton, and now Joseph Biden engaging in more targeted military activities, such as raids, bombings, or small-scale stabilization operations. Table 1.1 illustrates two things: first, that each president since Carter has either expressed intentions to do less in the Middle East or recognized that not being strategic enough about the Middle East has led to suboptimal results; and second, that despite these intentions, each administration since Carter has initiated new military activity in the region.

It is time to break this cycle through recognition of the full range of traditional and nontraditional U.S. security interests in the Middle East and through strategic, consistent, and coherent management of these issues with means that rely less on the U.S. military and more on the tools of diplomacy and economic engagement. In particular as the United States reconsiders its

---

[11] Brett McGurk, "The Cost of an Incoherent Foreign Policy: Trump's Iran Imbroglio Undermines U.S. Priorities Everywhere Else," *Foreign Affairs*, January 22, 2020.

TABLE 1.1

Key Military Activities in the Middle East Initiated or Conducted by U.S. Administrations

President	Each President's Intentions Prior to Military Intervention or Perspectives After Military Intervention	Key Military Activity
Carter	2014: "I think I would have been reelected easily if I had been able to rescue our hostages from the Iranians . . . And when that failed, then I think that was the main factor that brought about my failure to be reelected."[a]	In 1979, Iranian college students took 52 American diplomats hostage for 444 days in the Iran hostage crisis. Carter's launch of Operation Eagle Claw failed to rescue them. One reason for Carter's defeat for his second presidential term was this crisis.
Reagan	1990: "In the weeks immediately after the bombing, I believe the last thing that we should do was turn tail and leave. Yet the irrationality of Middle Eastern politics forced us to rethink our policy there. If there would be some rethinking of policy before our men die, we would be a lot better off. If that policy had changed towards more of a neutral position and neutrality, those 241 marines would be alive today."[b] 1986: "Long before I came into this office, Colonel Qaddafi had engaged in acts of international terror—acts that put him outside the company of civilized men. For years, however, he suffered no economic, or political or military sanction, and the atrocities mounted in number, as did the innocent dead and wounded."[c]	In 1982, the United States sent peacekeeping forces to Lebanon. In 1983, a suicide bombing of U.S. marine barracks in Beirut killed 241 military personnel, leading to withdrawal of U.S. and international peacekeeping forces. In response to support for terrorist activities and other provocations by Libyan president Muammar Gaddafi, the U.S. bombed Libya in 1986 in Operation El Dorado Canyon.
Bush (41)	1991: "I've told the American people before that this will not be another Vietnam, and I repeat this here tonight. Our troops will have the best possible support in the entire world, and they will not be asked to fight with one hand tied behind their back. I'm hopeful that this fighting will not go on for long and that casualties will be held to an absolute minimum."[d]	In response to Iraq's 1990 invasion of Kuwait, coalition forces of 35 countries led by the United States liberated Kuwait and advanced into Iraq. The Gulf War (1990–1991) aimed to secure energy supplies and included Operation Desert Shield and Operation Desert Storm; 700,000 U.S. troops took part.[e]

Table 1.1—Continued

President	Each President's Intentions Prior to Military Intervention or Perspectives After Military Intervention	Key Military Activity
Clinton	1993: "Throughout the Middle East, there is a great yearning for the quiet miracle of a normal life."[f]	From 1993 to 1998 (culminating in 1998 in Operation Desert Fox), the United States launched cruise missiles and other air attacks on Iraq in response to Iraqi aggression and positioned troops and equipment in Kuwait, Saudi Arabia, and Qatar.
Bush (43)	2003: "Major combat operations in Iraq have ended. In the Battle of Iraq, the United States and our allies have prevailed."[g]	After the September 11, 2001, attacks on the United States, the U.S. launched the Global War on Terrorism, with invasions of Afghanistan and Iraq in Operation Enduring Freedom (OEF) and Operation Iraqi Freedom (OIF). Major military operations continued through the end of the Bush administration.
Obama	2008: "When I am commander in chief, I will set a new goal on day one: I will end this war."[h] 2014: "(You) cannot, over the long term or even the medium term, deal with this problem by having the United States serially occupy various countries all around the Middle East. We don't have the resources. It puts enormous strains on our military. And at some point, we leave. And then things blow up again. So we've got to have a more sustainable strategy . . . The notion that the United States should be putting boots on the ground, I think would be a profound mistake. And I want to be very clear and very explicit about that."[i]	The United States withdrew its troops from Iraq in 2011, leaving conditions that enabled the rise of ISIS in 2014. In 2014, the United States sent troops back to Iraq and also provided air support in military operations against ISIS, as part of the Combined Joint Task-Force-Operation Inherent Resolve. The United States also sent conventional and special operations forces to Syria and conducted an air campaign there. In 2011 during Arab Spring uprisings in Libya, the North Atlantic Treaty Organization (NATO) conducted air strikes (with leading roles for the United States, the United Kingdom, and France) that supported the toppling of the Gaddafi regime. This led to ongoing civil war in Libya.
Trump	2016: "We don't want to have a depleted military because we're all over the place fighting in areas that we shouldn't be fighting in. It's not going to be depleted any longer."[j]	The United States continued the counter-ISIS campaign, with the territorial defeat of ISIS in Iraq in 2017 and in Syria in 2019.

Table 1.1—Continued

President	Each President's Intentions Prior to Military Intervention or Perspectives After Military Intervention	Key Military Activity
	2016: "Logic was replaced with foolishness and arrogance, which led to one foreign policy disaster after another. They just kept coming and coming. We went from mistakes in Iraq to Egypt to Libya, to President Obama's line in the sand in Syria. Each of these actions have helped to throw the region into chaos and gave ISIS the space it needs to grow and prosper."[k]	In 2019, the United States sent an additional 20,000 U.S. troops to the Middle East to counter Iran's activities and in response to attacks on American targets in Iraq. The United States assassinated Qasim Suleimani and Abu Mahdi Al-Muhanis in January 2020.
Biden	From joebiden.com in 2021: "Biden will end the forever wars in Afghanistan and the Middle East, which have cost us untold blood and treasure. . . . Biden will . . . narrowly focus our mission on Al-Qaeda and ISIS. And he will end our support for the Saudi-led war in Yemen. Staying entrenched in unwinnable conflicts only drains our capacity to lead on other issues that require our attention, and it prevents us from rebuilding the other instruments of American power."[l]	The United States conducted military strikes on Iranian-backed militias in Syria in February 2021 after rocket attacks on U.S. targets in Erbil, Iraq.

[a] Hunter Walker, "Jimmy Carter: 'I Could Have Wiped Iran Off the Map,'" *Business Insider*, October 1, 2014.

[b] Alan Bock, "Reagan's Wisdom on the Middle East: Leave," *Orange County Register*, July 21, 2006.

[c] Ronald Reagan, "Transcript of Address by Reagan on Libya," April 15, 1986.

[d] George H. W. Bush, "Address to the Nation on the Invasion of Iraq," speech, Washington, D.C.: The White House, January 16, 1991.

[e] Shannon Collins, "Desert Storm: A Look Back," *DoD News*, January 11, 2019.

[f] Bill Clinton, "Remarks at the Signing of the Israeli-Palestinian Agreement," video, Washington, D.C.: The White House, September 13, 1993.

[g] CBS News, "Text of Bush Speech," webpage, May 1, 2003.

[h] Edward Delman, "Obama Promised to End America's Wars—Has He?" *The Atlantic*, March 30, 2016.

[i] Gregory Korte, "Sixteen Times Obama Said There Would Be No Boots on the Ground in Syria," *USA Today*, October 31, 2015.

[j] McGurk, 2020.

[k] Ryan Teague Beckwith, "Read Donald Trump's 'America First' Foreign Policy Speech," *Time*, April 27, 2016.

[l] Biden for President, "The Power of America's Example: The Biden Plan for Leading the Democratic World to Meet the Challenges of the 21st Century," webpage, undated.

military footprint in the Middle East, it will need to manage its interests by using its other sources of power and not creating "fresh insecurity."[12]

A Changing Context in the Middle East Also Calls for New U.S. Security Approaches Toward the Region

In addition to the changing context in the United States, the Middle East political, security, and economic landscape is very different than it has been in recent decades. This means that U.S. national security interests in the region, and the risks posed to these interests, have evolved in ways that call for a modified set of priorities. Maintaining the same set of priorities and approaches from five, ten, or twenty years ago will not enable the United States to break its militarized relations in the Middle East or to address new threats or take advantage of new opportunities. Here are some of the most consequential changes.

The United States is not involved in major combat in the Middle East. For the first time in nearly two decades since 9/11, the United States is not involved in major combat operations in the Middle East. Instead, much as it has kept troops in Europe after World War II, when security threats from the Soviet Union were present, and in South Korea after the Korean War, in the absence of a peace agreement, it now has smaller numbers of troops in warzones with a limited mission set focused on counterterrorism and support of partners. Two thousand five hundred troops remain in Iraq, and 900 remain in Syria,[13] while the Biden administration pulled the remaining troops out of Afghanistan in September 2021. Notably, the remaining troop presence in the Middle East is smaller than in those other post-conflict settings. Total U.S. military personnel numbers in the Middle East are now less

---

[12] Daniel Benaim and Jake Sullivan, "America's Opportunity in the Middle East: Diplomacy Could Succeed Where Military Force Has Failed," *Foreign Affairs*, May 22, 2020.

[13] David S. Cloud, "Inside U.S. Troops' Stronghold in Syria, a Question of How Long Biden Will Keep Them There," *Los Angeles Times*, March 12, 2021; Jim Garamone, "U.S. Completes Troop-Level Drawdown in Afghanistan, Iraq," *DoD News*, January 15, 2021.

than 50,000, which is similar to Europe and Northeast Asia, with 60,000 to 80,000 each, out of a total 1.4 million active U.S. military personnel worldwide.[14]

Arab Spring sentiments are still at play. Ten years after the 2011 Arab Spring, civil wars resulting from the initial government overthrows rage on, and there have been few tangible improvements related to Arab Spring aspirations in most countries. However, the ideas of the movement have shaped aspirations and plans in ways that may play out in coming decades.[15] Protests in twelve countries during 2018–2021 and a spate of government vision documents show ongoing civil society demand for peaceful lives, better governance, and economic opportunities, along with government gestures to fulfill these demands. Of note is that mass protest movements have persisted not for utopian goals such as pan-Arabism or a restored caliphate, but for the simple desire to live a decent life with a good education, job opportunities, and personal safety, and without the constant scourge of government corruption.[16]

The COVID-19 pandemic will be a consideration for the next several years. While the United States and Europe see an end in sight, aiming to vaccinate their populations in 2021, the health and economic pressures of the pandemic will not let up elsewhere. Many countries, including most in the Middle East, are unlikely to have full vaccine rollout until 2023 or 2024.[17]

Relations with Iran are much worse. After the United States exited the 2015 Iran nuclear deal, the Joint Comprehensive Plan of Action (JCPOA), and instituted a "maximum pressure" campaign complete with restored and even new sanctions, Iran started violating the terms of the deal, surpassing the agreed limits of its stockpile of low-enriched uranium, and suspending

---

[14] Lubold and Strobel, 2021; International Institute for Strategic Studies, *The Military Balance 2021*, London, February 2021.

[15] Shelly Culbertson, *The Fires of Spring: A Post–Arab Spring Journey Through the Turbulent New Middle East*, New York: St. Martin's Press, 2016.

[16] Culbertson, 2016.

[17] Saeed Shah, Gabriele Steinhauser, and Feliz Solomon, "Vaccine Delays in Developing Nations Risk Prolonging Pandemic," *Wall Street Journal*, February 17, 2021.

international snap inspections of undeclared nuclear sites.[18] Iranian affiliated militias in Iraq and Syria have fired missiles at U.S. bases, prompting President Biden to conduct a military strike in retaliation just over a month into the new administration.

There are many festering conflicts without clear prospects for near-term resolution. Civil wars are ongoing in Syria, Yemen, and Libya. Tensions are at play around gas rights in the Eastern Mediterranean. Tensions are reduced but remain between Qatar and other countries in the Gulf. Many countries of the region view Iran's actions as the greatest threat, with the Abraham Accords that normalized relations between Israel and several Arab countries illustrating a realignment of Arab countries and Israel against Iran.

The Israeli-Palestinian conflict is no longer the epicenter of Middle East tensions. Even before the May 2021 exchange of rocket attacks and airstrikes between Israel and Gaza, the prospects for a peace agreement between the Israelis and Palestinians were dim, as the parties failed to reach an agreement despite the efforts of successive U.S. presidents in recent decades. Yet the region's many conflicts, in addition to more Arab countries normalizing relations with Israel in the Abraham Accords, means that it is now just one of several conflicts. Resolving this conflict is no longer the main prerequisite for other regional initiatives; U.S. approaches toward this have evolved toward conflict management instead of conflict resolution.[19]

The Middle East has become a theater for great and regional power competition. The United States is no longer the only great power engaging in the Middle East. China and Russia are more active, competing with the United States for influence through weapons sales, economic investment, military engagement, and diplomacy. Turkey is increasingly wielding its influence and military power. Iran and Saudi Arabia fuel proxy warfare in multiple countries.[20]

[18] U.S. Institute of Peace, "Biden & Iran: The Nuclear Deal," *The Iran Primer*, updated March 9, 2021.

[19] Michael Crowley, "Violence in Israel Challenges Biden's 'Stand Back' Approach," *New York Times*, May 11, 2021.

[20] Kim Ghattas, *Black Wave: Saudi Arabia, Iran, and the Forty-Year Rivalry that Unraveled Culture, Religion, and Collective Memory in the Middle East*, New York: Henry Holt

There are successes to build upon and assets to protect. The problems in the region should not obscure the successes, positive developments, and opportunities. The United States can build upon these. Recent years have seen the defeat of ISIS as a territorial power by the Iraqi military and the Syrian Democratic Forces with American and multinational support, the Abraham Accords, and positive effects of American military security cooperation efforts. Other positive developments include slowly improving education systems, greater rights for women, the dynamism of the growing youth population, prosperity in the Gulf, widespread use of information technology, development of country-level visions, improvements in health, a small but growing culture of innovation, and engagement of civil society and youth.[21]

Approach and Roadmap to This Report

This report relied on an extensive literature review, a series of consultations with researchers at RAND with expertise in related topics, and expert perspective of the authors. The literature review included academic literature, policy research literature, government reports, and popular media. We also reviewed public data sources (such as about energy and trade). To develop our discussion of U.S. interests, we considered core interests that have stood the test of time through politically different administrations. We then considered regional characteristics that have caused notable problems for the United States and added them to interests that needed to be addressed. Then to develop the recommendations, we looked at changes in both the United States and the Middle East that create new circumstances or opportunities.

After this introduction, we offer a new conceptualization of U.S. broad security interests in the Middle East through a "top-ten" list. We then offer recommendations for renewing U.S. security strategy in the region.

---

and Company, 2020.

[21] For more on the Middle Eastern technology and innovation scene, see Christopher M. Schroeder, *Startup Rising: The Entrepreneurial Revolution Remaking the Middle East*, New York: St. Martin's Press, 2013, as well as Schroeder's more recent columns in his newsletter, *Seeking Awesome*.

CHAPTER 2

A Top-Ten List of U.S. Security Interests in the Middle East

Recognizing the changing political, security, and economic contexts in both the United States and the Middle East, we present a proposed top-ten list of security issues in the Middle East that require ongoing U.S. engagement and management. These include the three traditional U.S. security interests—namely, terrorism, energy, and nuclear nonproliferation—as well as nontraditional security issues that have risen to the fore. The following security issues interact in ways that demand a more integrated U.S. approach to managing them:

- preventing terrorism
- protecting global energy markets
- ensuring nuclear nonproliferation
- staying ahead in great power competition
- mitigating regional aggression and conflicts
- lowering human and financial costs to manage U.S. interests
- addressing forced displacement
- mitigating climate change impacts
- protecting the security and economic well-being of U.S. allies and partners
- promoting societies with the rule of law and economic opportunities.

Terrorist Groups Are Degraded, but They Still Have Capabilities

The United States has undertaken two decades of military operations to combat violent extremist groups in the greater Middle East, including the invasions of Afghanistan and Iraq after September 11, subsequent counter-insurgency operations that involved large-scale military presence, operations against ISIS in Iraq and Syria, and airstrikes targeting leaders of terrorist organizations.[1] However, despite the success of these operations, risks of violent extremism still require ongoing U.S. engagement. Military means alone will not be sufficient to address these risks, which will also require other tools: diplomacy, community engagement, law enforcement, education, and improvement of governance and economic conditions. Violent extremism remains a global risk—not just a risk to the region—that will continue to rely on U.S. engagement for several reasons.

Many of the terrorist movements that the United States has targeted either still exist or have evolved into different organizations. Although they operate at lower levels than recent decades, they still have the affiliates, resources, and will to cause problems for the United States and its allies and partners. ISIS is estimated to have 11,000 to 18,000 affiliated individuals in Iraq and Syria, with roughly 1,000 more in Libya, Sinai, and Yemen.[2] The U.S. Department of the Treasury estimates that ISIS still has $100 million at its disposal.[3] This is enough to maintain a low-grade insurgency. Al-Qaeda retains an estimated 10,000 to 20,000 affiliated individuals, centered in Yemen and Syria.[4] History has shown the consequences of neglecting such risks; U.S. withdrawal from Iraq in 2011 left a vacuum that enabled the rise of ISIS as a territorial power, which pulled the United States into war to defeat the group.[5]

---

[1] DoD, "Separate U.S. Airstrikes Kill 2 Senior al-Qaida Leaders in Syria," *DOD News*, January 17, 2017.

[2] Aaron Zelin and Michael Knights, *The Islamic State's Resurgence in the COVID Era? From Defeat to Renewal in Iraq and Syria*, Washington, D.C.: Washington Institute for Near East Policy, May 29, 2020.

[3] Gregory Sullivan, Audit Director, "Operation Inherent Resolve—Summary of Work Performed by the Department of the Treasury Related to Terrorist Financing, ISIS, and Anti-Money Laundering for First Quarter Fiscal Year 2021," memorandum to Department of Defense Lead Inspector General, Washington, D.C., January 4, 2021.

[4] Cameron Glenn, Mattisan Rowan, John Caves, and Garrett Nada, "Timeline: The Rise, Spread, and Fall of the Islamic State," Washington, D.C.: The Wilson Center, October 28, 2019.

[5] Ben Connable, James Dobbins, Howard J. Shatz, Raphael S. Cohen, and Becca Wasser, *Weighing U.S. Troop Withdrawal from Iraq: Strategic Risks and Recommendations*, Santa Monica, Calif.: RAND Corporation, PE-362-OSD, 2020.

There is no solution being implemented for what to do with detained ISIS fighters and their families in Syria, and this poses future risks for violence if the issue is not addressed. The approximately 10,000 ISIS detainees held in northern Syria are a major security concern.[6] To date, mass breakouts have not yet occurred; however, a potential prison break could galvanize a resurgence in violent extremist activity, as was the case with Iraq's Abu Ghraib prison in 2013 and other breakouts around that time.[7] In addition, the ISIS family members (wives and children) who are held in camps in Syria where they are mixed in with displaced civilians, such as in the Al-Hol camp, present security and radicalization threats. Complex issues related to their future—including justice procedures, whether the foreigners can return to their home countries, and how they will be detained securely— have not been worked out. A generation of this group of children is growing up in squalid camps, surrounded by extremist ideology.[8]

There is still some popular support for violent extremism in the Middle East and North Africa. The 2018 Arab Youth Survey and the 2019–2020 Arab Opinion Index both found that 88 percent of survey participants viewed ISIS negatively, a number that has increased every year since 2014, with the remainder expressing support or neutrality.[9] ISIS may never have had a large percentage of support, but a small percentage of a large population is a large number of people. Yet, it is important to note that positive

---

[6] Richard Barrett, *Beyond the Caliphate: Foreign Fighters and the Threat of Returnees*, New York: Soufan Group, October 2017, p. 20; Inspector General, *Operation Inherent Resolve: Lead Inspector General Report to the United States Congress*, Washington, D.C., July 1, 2020–September 30, 2020b, p. 55; Aaron Y. Zelin, *Wilayat al-Hawl: 'Remaining' and Incubating the Next Islamic State Generation*, Washington, D.C.: Washington Institute for Near East Policy, October 18, 2019.

[7] Martin Chulov, "ISIS: The Inside Story," *The Guardian*, December 11, 2014; Brian Michael Jenkins, "Options for Dealing with Islamic State Foreign Fighters Currently Detained in Syria," *CTC Sentinel*, Vol. 12, No. 5, May/June 2019; and Eric Oehlerich, Mick Mulroy, and Liam McHugh, *Jannah or Jahannam: Options for Dealing with ISIS Detainees*, Washington, D.C.: Middle East Institute, October 2020.

[8] International Crisis Group, "Exiles in Their Own Country: Dealing with Displacement in Post-ISIS Iraq," Briefing No. 79, October 19, 2020.

[9] ASDA'A BCW, *Arab Youth Survey: A Decade of Hopes and Fears*, 2018; Arab Center Washington D.C., "The 2019–2020 Arab Opinion Index: Main Results in Brief," webpage, November 16, 2020.

views of extremist groups do not equate to violent extremist action. The process of radicalization involves a transition from supporting to abetting, conducting, or promoting terrorist acts.

There is no consensus yet on exactly how radicalization happens, although some studies find this more likely in nondemocratic and unstable countries with high antigovernment sentiment; they also find that poor economic conditions alone are not likely to lead to radicalization or terrorist activity.[10] Many of the underlying conditions that lead to support for violent extremism in the Middle East still exist or are worse than earlier waves of radicalization that led to the growth of Al-Qaeda and ISIS. Ongoing conflict in, and fragility of, multiple states in the region—namely, Syria, Iraq, Yemen, Lebanon, and Libya—have created space for extremist groups to survive. Indeed, a recent Lead Inspector General report on Operation Inherent Resolve, the U.S. government's counter-ISIS mission, affirmed that "unless the root causes of ISIS's proliferation are addressed—such as ineffective governance and service delivery, lack of economic opportunity, and sectarian division—the group would continue to regenerate."[11]

Beyond addressing root causes, any effort to counter violent extremism will need to take account of how people become radicalized, not just why they are attracted. In this context, the most important vector for recruitment currently is information technology and social media, where online communities can serve as sources of inspiration and means for recruitment.[12] ISIS has been adept at exploiting social media and other online platforms for recruiting purposes.[13]

---

[10] Richard C. Baffa, Nathan Vest, Wing Yi Chan, and Abby Fanlo, *Defining and Understanding the Next Generation of Salafi-Jihadis*, Santa Monica, Calif.: RAND Corporation, PE-341-ODNI, 2019, p. 3; Tim Krieger and Daniel Meierrieks, "What Causes Terrorism?" *Public Choice*, Vol. 147, No. 1/2, April 2011, p. 19; Nate Rosenblatt, *All Jihad Is Local: What ISIS' Files Tell Us About Its Fighters*, Washington, D.C.: New America, July 20, 2016.

[11] Inspector General, *Operation Inherent Resolve: Lead Inspector General Report to the United States Congress*, Washington, D.C., April 1, 2020–June 30, 2020a, p. 20.

[12] DoD, *Summary of the 2018 National Defense Strategy of the United States of America: Sharpening the American Military's Competitive Edge*, Washington, D.C., January 20, 2018.

[13] Charlie Winter, Shiraz Maher, and Aymenn Jawad al-Tamimi, *Understand Salafi-Jihadist Attitudes Towards Innovation*, London: International Centre for the Study of Radicalisation, 2021, p. 3.

While the United States Now Relies Less on Middle East Energy, Its Allies Still Depend on It

The United States has served as a guarantor of the stability of global energy markets since shortly after World War II. As long as oil and gas remain important to the global economy, the United States will continue to need to play its guarantor role, because even though it does not currently rely significantly on Middle East energy, Asian and European allies of the United States do. A reduced American role would leave a vacuum that could strengthen the leverage of Russia and China over these allies.

The Middle East remains a dominant provider of oil and gas globally. In 2019, the countries of the Middle East and North Africa accounted for 51.8 percent of the world's oil reserves and were responsible for 35.5 percent of total world production.[14] They accounted for 42.0 percent of the world's gas reserves and produced 56.8 percent of the world total. These natural gas reserves and outputs are likely to go up as new gas fields in the Mediterranean are developed.[15]

This U.S. role in Middle East energy can be traced back to the relationship that developed between the United States and Saudi Arabia during World War II, when President Franklin D. Roosevelt declared in 1943 that "the defense of Saudi Arabia is vital to the defense of the United States."[16] The United States took a further step toward defense of global energy supplies with the so-called Carter Doctrine, with President Carter saying in 1980 that "an attempt by any outside force to gain control of the Persian Gulf region will be regarded as an assault on the vital interests of the United States of America, and such an assault will be repelled by any

---

[14] British Petroleum, *Statistical Review of World Energy 2020*, 69th ed., London, June 2020.

[15] John V. Bowlus, "Eastern Mediterranean Gas: Testing the Field," in *Deep Sea Rivals: Europe, Turkey, and New Eastern Mediterranean Conflict Lines*, London: European Council on Foreign Relations, May 2020.

[16] Jimmy H. Howard, *The United States and Saudi Arabia: A Special Relationship; Its Birth, Evolution and Reapportionment*, thesis, Monterey, Calif.: Naval Postgraduate School, June 1981.

means necessary, including military force."[17] This defense of energy supplies became concrete in the so-called Tanker War during the Iran-Iraq War of 1980–1988; the 1990–1991 Gulf War, sparked by Iraq's invasion of Kuwait and fears for the security of Saudi oil fields; and the United States' pledge, in light of Iranian maritime provocations, to guarantee safe passage of commercial shipping through the Strait of Hormuz as part of Operational Sentinel.[18]

The United States does not currently depend heavily on the Middle East for its energy. In 2019, only 13 percent of all U.S. imports of crude petroleum and petroleum products came from the Middle East.[19] In addition, U.S. petroleum exports were 93 percent of U.S. petroleum imports, suggesting even less of a need for Middle Eastern oil should an emergency arise.[20]

In contrast, U.S. allies depend heavily on Middle Eastern energy. This is especially true of Asian allies and partners. Although China's heavy dependence on Middle Eastern oil can raise the question of why the United States should be safeguarding global energy supplies, U.S. treaty allies also depend heavily on the Middle East for their energy, as does much of the rest of Asia. A diminished U.S. role in global energy markets could leave Asia, and Asian allies, more dependent on China, which would work counter to the overall U.S. strategy of safeguarding against Chinese dominance in Asia.[21] For

---

[17] The statement came in response to two events in 1979: an oil shock following the Iranian revolution of 1979, and then the Soviet invasion of Afghanistan in December 1979, which raised fears the Soviet Union could move closer to the Strait of Hormuz, through which most of the world oil exports flowed (Jimmy Carter, *The State of the Union Address Delivered Before a Joint Session of the Congress*, Washington, D.C.: The White House, January 23, 1980).

[18] C. Todd Lopez, *Esper: Operation Sentinel Prevents Escalation of Middle East Waterways Conflict*, Washington, D.C.: U.S. Department of Defense, July 24, 2019.

[19] U.S. Energy Information Administration (EIA), "U.S. Total Crude Oil and Products Imports," Excel file, January 29, 2021b.

[20] EIA, "Total Crude Oil and Products Exports by Destination," Excel file, January 29, 2021c.

[21] Jon B. Alterman, "Pivoting to Asia Doesn't Get You Out of the Middle East," Washington, D.C.: Center for Strategic and International Studies, October 19, 2020.

example, in 2019, Japan received almost 90 percent of its crude oil imports from the Middle East and North Africa, constituting 75 percent of Japan's total petroleum consumption.[22] This allied dependence on the Middle East for energy is one component of great power competition in the Middle East, discussed below.

While Europe currently relies heavily on Russian gas imports, in the future, Europe could start relying more heavily on the Eastern Mediterranean gas fields. Middle Eastern exports already provided 47 percent of consumption in Spain, 35 percent in Italy, and 27 percent in Belgium.[23] The United States has an interest in reducing Europe's use of Russia's gas—as does Europe—and the ability to tap Mediterranean gas reserves has been moving forward, for example in an agreement between Israel, Cyprus, and Greece regarding the so-called EastMed Pipeline.[24] In addition, U.S. military forces are not necessarily needed to safeguard supply, as relevant European and Middle Eastern countries have effective navies, but a U.S. backup can be useful to support regional navies.

Over the longer term, as a transition to lower use of carbon-intensive energy sources occurs, the Middle East's importance as an energy supplier to the global economy may recede, and with it global interest in the region. However, that time is likely far off. According to U.S. Energy Information Administration (EIA) projections, the share of renewables in primary energy consumption may rise from 15 percent in 2018 to 28 percent in 2050, but during the same period, the share of petroleum and other liquids is projected to fall from 32 percent to a still-high 27 percent, and the share of natural gas is projected to stay about 22 percent, so that hydrocarbons will still serve as the source of almost half of the world's energy consumption. And in both cases, the amount used is expected to increase, meaning the Middle East will remain important as an energy supplier.[25]

---

[22] British Petroleum, 2020.

[23] British Petroleum, 2020.

[24] Scott Carpenter, "New Pipeline Deal Gives Europe Access to Eastern Mediterranean Gas Reserves, Angering Turkey," *Forbes*, January 2, 2020; Angeliki Koutantou, "Greece, Israel, Cyprus Sign EastMed Gas Pipeline Deal," Reuters, January 2, 2020.

[25] EIA, *International Energy Outlook 2019*, Washington, D.C., September 24, 2019.

The Middle East Is a Hot Spot for Nuclear Proliferation Threats

Stopping the proliferation of nuclear weapons in the Middle East remains an important U.S. interest and is part of broader, longstanding U.S. efforts to halt proliferation worldwide, beyond countries that already have nuclear capabilities.[26] In the Middle East, the nonproliferation issue focuses mainly, but not exclusively, on Iran. Fears that should Iran gain nuclear weapons, other countries, such as Saudi Arabia, will follow extends the scope of U.S. interest.[27] Turkey, too, is a country considered possible in terms of attempting to gain a nuclear weapon, regardless of Iran's actions.[28] Other countries previously appeared to have nuclear arms programs including Iraq, Libya and Syria, but no longer do so.[29]

The United States has tried two broad strategies for halting the Iranian nuclear bomb and is now embarked on what could be a third. In broad-brush terms, the first, which came to fruition during the Obama era, started with negotiations in 2006 between Iran and six major powers (the five permanent members of the UN Security Council plus Germany), moved to globally coordinated sanctions, continued with negotiations, and concluded with the JCPOA in 2015, effective in 2016. In return for a variety of Iranian commitments related to nuclear weapons and facilities, the United States

---

[26] Committee on Nuclear Proliferation, *A Report to the President by the Committee on Nuclear Proliferation*, Washington, D.C., January 21, 1965.

[27] Norah O'Donnell, "Saudi Crown Prince: If Iran Develops Nuclear Bomb, So Will We," CBS TV, March 15, 2018.

[28] John Spacapan, "Conventional Wisdom Says That TurkeyWon't Go Nuclear. That Might Be Wrong," *Bulletin of the Atomic Scientists*, July 7, 2020; Douglas Little, "The Making of a Special Relationship: The United States and Israel, 1957–68," *International Journal of Middle East Studies*, Vol. 25, No. 4, November 1993, pp. 563–585. More recently, Iran has routinely called for Israel to be destroyed or claimed it had the capacity to do so, but usually has not said directly that it would do so ("Top Iran General Says Destroying Israel 'Achievable Goal,'" *VOA News*, September 30, 2019; Josh Levs, "Iran Leader's Call to 'Annihilate' Israel Sparks Fury as Nuclear Deadline Looms," CNN, November 10, 2014; and Amir Vahdat and Jon Gambrell, "Iran Leader Says Israel a 'Cancerous Tumor' to Be Destroyed," AP, May 22, 2020).

[29] Arms Control Association, "Nuclear Weapons: Who Has What at a Glance," Fact Sheets and Briefs, August 2020.

and the rest of the world eased sanctions, but the United States did not remove them entirely, as it had sanctions programs related to other issues.[30] Of note is that the United States' regional partners and allies—those most at risk from an Iranian nuclear weapon—were unhappy with the terms of the nuclear agreement and made clear that they felt that they had been unnecessarily excluded from negotiations.[31]

The Trump administration implemented the second strategy. Despite general agreement that Iran was complying with the nuclear accord, the administration said that the accord did not adequately deal with the potential for an Iranian nuclear weapon, in part by being time limited, and that it entirely ignored Iran's other malign activities.[32] Accordingly, the United States withdrew in 2018 and reinstituted sanctions in what it termed a "maximum pressure" campaign. Some regional partners said they agreed with this decision.[33] Stated goals were to negotiate a deal that encompassed the range of Iranian activities that the United States found to be security threats.

Although the renewed sanctions caused great economic damage to Iran, Iran did not return to the negotiating table and started breeching some of its obligations under the nuclear agreement. Accordingly, the Biden administration started to move forward with a third strategy.

The Biden administration has committed to rejoining the agreement and as of May 2020 had embarked on indirect talks, mediated by the other

---

[30] Paul K. Kerr and Kenneth Katzman, *Iran Nuclear Agreement and U.S. Exit*, Washington, D.C.: Congressional Research Service, R43333, July 20, 2018.

[31] Israel firmly opposed the deal. Saudi Arabia was unhappy with the deal, but did not firmly oppose it publicly. See Isabel Kershner, "Iran Deal Denounced by Netanyahu as 'Historic Mistake,'" *New York Times*, July 14, 2015; Loveday Morris and Hugh Naylor, "Arab States Fear Nuclear Deal Will Give Iran a Bigger Regional Role," *Washington Post*, July 14, 2015.

[32] On compliance, see Paul K. Kerr, *Iran's Nuclear Program: Tehran's Compliance with International Obligations*, Washington, D.C.: Congressional Research Service, R40094, November 20, 2020.

[33] Embassy of the United Arab Emirates, "UAE Supports US President's Decision to Withdraw from Iranian Nuclear Agreement," Washington, D.C., undated; Ghaida Ghantous, Stephen Kalin, and Sarah Dadouch, "Saudi Arabia Says Backs U.S. Decision to Withdraw from Iran Nuclear Deal," Reuters, May 8, 2018.

JCPOA partners.[34] But at least three important issues are on the table. The first concerns which sanctions the United States will remove. The second involves other, nonnuclear Iranian security challenges, such as those related to Iran's missile programs and regional activities.[35] The third issue is the treatment of regional allies and partners this time around. France, for one, had reportedly said that Saudi Arabia must be involved in any new talks.[36]

There is a final issue that makes an evaluation of any nuclear deal difficult. Iran has shown during the period of maximum pressure that it is willing to weather hardships. The change of U.S. administrations cut that effort short by four years, presuming a second Trump administration would have extended it, so there is no way to know whether it could have forced a chastened Iran back to the negotiating table. More sobering, however, is the extent to which any agreement can ultimately stop Iran from creating a nuclear weapon if it really wants one.[37] Accordingly, even if there is a renewed deal, any Iran nuclear policy will need to consider containment as well. And as before, the role of allies and partners will be prominent in such a calculation.

The Middle East Is a Theater for Great Power Competition

As of the beginning of President Biden's term, great power competition with peer and near-peer rivals China and Russia remains the centerpiece of U.S. security policy. The Biden administration's Interim National Security Strategic Guidance focuses the competition on China and builds on the

---

[34] Daphne Psaledakis and Arshad Mohammed, "U.S. Tiptoes Through Sanctions Minefield Toward Iran Nuclear Deal," Reuters, May 17, 2021.

[35] U.S. Department of State, "Joint Statement by the Secretary of State of the United States of America and the Foreign Ministers of France, Germany, and the United Kingdom," Media Note, Washington, D.C.: Office of the Spokesperson, February 18, 2021.

[36] Mohammed Al-Kinani, "Saudi Arabia Must Be Involved in Fresh Talks on Iran Deal, Says Macron," Arab News, January 29, 2021.

[37] Robert Reardon, Containing Iran: Strategies for Addressing the Iranian Nuclear Challenge, Santa Monica, Calif.: RAND Corporation, MG-1180-TSF, 2012.

premise in the Trump-era National Defense Strategy that China and Russia are the "central challenge to U.S. prosperity and security."[38]

Competition will not occur solely in the near-abroad of great powers, and the Middle East will remain important to this competition. None of the three major powers has the same goals. Even if neither China nor Russia is trying to supplant the United States' dominant role in the Middle East, both have some objectives in the region that run counter to U.S. interests. U.S. disengagement would risk allowing Russia and China to pursue these objectives unchallenged. Furthermore, greater Chinese dominance in the region could negatively affect U.S. allies and partners. Not only do the United States' Asian allies depend on the region for energy, but it is also an essential link in trade with Europe, and China's dominance in the region could enable it to extend its influence further in Asia.

While the United States is trying to reduce its military footprint, China is trying to extend its economic reach without either alienating partners or getting drawn in militarily, and Russia is seeking opportunities to advance its security and economic interests and global profile, as well as opportunities to foil the United States. In this way, many of the actions and goals of the three powers are asymmetrical, but actions by each can affect the other in broader great power competition. U.S. retrenchment from the Middle East would create opportunities for China and Russia to strengthen and extend their spheres of influence.

China's main interests in the region are economic, as it has become a top trading partner and investor. China's activities in the Middle East have made it an "economic heavyweight," a "diplomatic lightweight," and a "military featherweight."[39] China relies heavily on Middle Eastern oil, and oil exporters depend on China as a large and growing customer in contrast to falling demand from the United States and Europe.[40] Through the Belt and Road

---

[38] The White House, 2021c; DoD, *Summary of the 2018 National Defense Strategy of the United States of America: Sharpening the American Military's Competitive Edge*, Washington, D.C., January 20, 2018.

[39] Andrew Scobell and Alireza Nader, *China in the Middle East: The Wary Dragon*, Santa Monica, Calif.: RAND Corporation, RR-1229-A, 2016.

[40] Jon B. Alterman, "Chinese and Russian Influence in the Middle East," statement before the House Foreign Affairs Subcommittee on the Middle East, North Africa, and

Initiative, China has expanded its role in Middle East infrastructure projects, such as by financing and building ports and telecommunications systems. It has furnished COVID-19 vaccines. China has become a top trading partner and investor for the region.[41] In 2018, China was the largest identified single-country goods trading partner for six countries in the Middle East.[42] China has also been working to expand its technological footprint. Recently, several Gulf Cooperation Council countries partnered with Huawei in deploying their 5G networks, against the wishes of the United States, which cited concerns that Huawei devices can be surveilled by the Chinese government.[43]

As a "diplomatic lightweight" and "military featherweight" in the region, China has proceeded cautiously, seeking to remain on good terms with all regional actors. Beijing maintains that its diplomacy is grounded in nonintervention in other countries' internal affairs.[44] These tenets, China hopes, will both make it a more appealing partner than the United States or European countries that condition aid on human rights and other interests and dissuade outside criticism of its own internal affairs, particularly in the context of its own poor treatment of Muslim minority groups domestically.[45] Although China has entered into what it calls strategic and comprehensive strategic partnerships with countries in the Middle East, it does not seem

---

International Terrorism, Washington, D.C.: Center for Strategic and International Studies, May 9, 2019; Camille Lons, Jonathan Fulton, Degang Sun, and Naser Al-Tamimi, *China's Great Game in the Middle East*, London: European Council on Foreign Relations, 2019.

[41] Ali Wyne and Colin P. Clarke, "Assessing China and Russia's Moves in the Middle East," *Lawfare*, September 17, 2020.

[42] United Nations, *UN Comtrade Database*, Online Database, Department of Economic and Social Affairs, Statistics Division, Trade Statistics, 2021.

[43] Mohammed Soliman, "The GCC, US-China Tech War, and the Next 5G Storm," Washington, D.C.: The Middle East Institute, September 1, 2020.

[44] The State Council, The People's Republic of China, "Full Text: China and the World in the New Era," webpage, September 27, 2019.

[45] Scobell and Nader, 2016, p. 20; David Schenker, "China and Russia: The New Threats to Middle East Security and Stability," remarks given to the Atlantic Council, Washington, D.C.: U.S. Department of State, October 8, 2019.

keen to escalate its military involvement, aside from opening its first overseas military base in Djibouti and modest but growing weapons sales.[46]

Russia's presence in the Middle East skews toward diplomatic and military engagement, and although it does not have the economic heft of China or the United States, it seeks economic engagement as opportunity allows. Russia tries to present itself as a steadfast partner, complicate U.S. objectives, and sell its military hardware.[47]

Russian military activities in the Middle East center on interventions on behalf of the Assad regime.[48] Despite Russia's stated objective of fighting terrorism, many of its strikes in Syria were carried out against U.S.-backed opposition groups.[49] As it props up a friendly regime, Russia has also managed to "throw sand in [America's] gears," as General Kenneth McKenzie Jr. put it, and to "appear to be a player on the global stage when it comes to Middle Eastern issues."[50] Russia's backing of Assad has been rewarded with access to an air base and a renewed lease on a naval logistics facility.[51] The Syrian regime granted lucrative deals to a Russian oligarch close to Putin for energy infrastructure, logistics, and the operation of a phosphate mine.[52] Russia has also asserted itself as an important outside actor in Libya.[53]

---

[46] Alterman, 2019; John Calabrese, "Intersections: China and the U.S. in the Middle East," Washington, D.C.: Middle East Institute, June 18, 2019; Lons et al., 2019; and Scobell and Nader, 2016.

[47] Michael Singh, *U.S. Policy in the Middle East amid Great Power Competition*, Beaver Creek, Colo.: Reagan Institute Strategy Group, 2020b.

[48] William F. Wechsler, "U.S. Withdrawal from the Middle East: Perceptions and Reality," in Karim Mezran and Arturo Varvelli, eds., *The MENA Region: A Great Power Competition*, Milan: ISPI and the Atlantic Council, 2019, pp. 13–38.

[49] Charles Lister, "After Five Years of Russian Intervention in Syria," *Asharq Al-Awsat*, August 15, 2020.

[50] Wyne and Clarke, 2020.

[51] Colin P. Clarke, William Courtney, Bradley Martin, and Bruce McClintock, "Russia Is Eyeing the Mediterranean. The U.S. and NATO Must Be Prepared," *The RAND Blog*, June 30, 2020.

[52] Chloe Cornish, Asser Khattab, and Henry Foy, "Moscow Collects Its Spoils of War in Assad's Syria," *Financial Times*, September 1, 2019.

[53] Lister, 2020.

Weapons sales in the Middle East remain a major component of Russia's presence in the region. As Russian arms sales decrease elsewhere in the world, Russia has turned to the Middle East to offset the decline and the growing gap between U.S. and Russian arms sales.[54] To this end, Russia supplied almost 20 percent of the arms imports for the region between 2015 and 2019; this represented a 30-percent increase over its exports to the region between 2010 and 2014.[55] Russia sells to U.S. partners and adversaries alike: Egypt and Iraq are the largest importers of Russian weapons, but Syria has heavily relied on Russia to obtain its weapons in the past, and with the expiration of the UN arms embargo on Iran, the prospect opens for Russia to sell to Tehran.[56] In selling to U.S. adversaries—such as Iran—Russia can help fuel destabilizing conflicts, and in selling to U.S. partners and allies— such as NATO ally Turkey—Russia can erode or at least strain the strategic relationship.[57] Even if it is not the central goal of Russia's Middle East policy, undermining U.S. interests is a welcome by-product.

Similar to China, Russia has maintained generally amicable relations with all countries in the region, even those on opposing sides of rivalries and conflicts.[58] The consistency of Russia's amicable relations, especially

---

[54] Alexey Khlebnikov, "Russia Looks to the Middle East to Boost Arms Exports," Washington, D.C.: Middle East Institute, April 8, 2019.

[55] Clayton Thomas, Jeremy Sharp, Christopher M. Blanchard, and Christina L. Arabia, *Arms Sales in the Middle East: Trends and Analytical Perspectives for U.S. Policy*, Washington, D.C.: Congressional Research Service, November 23, 2020, p. 2; Pieter D. Wezeman, Aude Fleurant, Alexandra Kuimova, Diego Lopes da Silva, Nan Tian, and Siemon T. Wezeman, "Trends in International Arms Transfers, 2019," SIPRI Fact Sheet, Stockholm: Stockholm International Peace Research Institute, March 2020, p. 4.

[56] Wezeman et al., 2020, p. 4; Paul Holtom, Mark Bromley, Pieter D. Wezeman, and Siemon T. Wezeman, "Trends in International Arms Transfers, 2012," SIPRI Fact Sheet, Stockholm: Stockholm International Peace Research Institute, March 2013, p. 8; Arman Mahmoudian and Giorgio Cafiero, "Does Russia Really Want a U.S. Return to the Iran Deal?" *IranSource*, January 19, 2021.

[57] Gönül Tol and Ömer Taşpınar, "Turkey's Russian Roulette," in Karim Mezran and Arturo Varvelli, eds., *The MENA Region: A Great Power Competition*, Milan: ISPI and Atlantic Council, 2019, p. 108.

[58] Mark N. Katz, "Same Ends but Different Means: Change, Continuity and Moscow's Middle East Policy," in Karim Mezran and Arturo Varvelli, eds., *The MENA Region: A Great Power Competition*, Milan: ISPI and Atlantic Council, 2019, p. 46.

when coupled with the perception of wavering American interest, offers another way through which Russia can build influence.[59] Russia has leveraged these relations to position itself as a potential mediator, most notably in the Astana Process, where its ties to multiple sides of the Syria conflict helped it arrange peace talks.

At the same time, another consideration in great power competition in general is that the United States faces a global drop in soft power, as opinions of the United States as a trusted partner and a society to emulate have declined.[60] In particular, a 2017 Pew survey found only a quarter of those surveyed in the Middle East had positive opinions about the United States; this was lower than positive opinions about Russia (a third).[61]

There are a number of fronts on which U.S. interests clash with those of Russia and China or where Russia and China are working to present themselves as alternatives to the United States. Militarily, Russia presents more of a challenge than China. Through its "anti-interventionist interventions,"[62] Russia is trying to carve out a role for itself in shaping the post-conflict conditions of the states in which it is involved. Russia does not seem intent on overtaking the United States as the main outside actor, but it may take advantage of opportunities to increase threats to the West originating in the Middle East.[63] China is similarly not pursuing the United States' role in the region; in fact, it benefits from free-riding off of the regional stability provided by U.S. military presence.[64] However, the possibility that China may increase its military

---

[59] Andrey Kortunov, "The Astana Model: Methods and Ambitions of Russian Political Action," in Karim Mezran and Arturo Varvelli, eds., *The MENA Region: A Great Power Competition*, Milan: ISPI and Atlantic Council, 2019, p. 54.

[60] James Dobbins, Gabrielle Tarini, and Ali Wyne, *The Lost Generation in American Foreign Policy*, Santa Monica, Calif.: RAND Corporation, PE-A232-1, 2020.

[61] Janell Fetterolf and Jacob Poushter, *Key Middle East Publics See Russia, Turkey and U.S. All Playing Larger Roles in Region*, Washington, D.C.: Pew Research Center, December 11, 2017.

[62] Lister, 2020.

[63] Singh, 2020b.

[64] Jon B. Alterman, *The Other Side of the World: China, the United States, and the Struggle for Middle East Security*, Washington, D.C.: Center for Strategic and International Studies, March 2017.

engagement in the future cannot be ruled out, especially if it one day finds that economic tools are insufficient to protect its deepening interests in the region. As Russia and China are not keen to question other countries' track records on human rights and governance, choosing to work with them over the United States in some contexts may appeal to countries that are wary of U.S. promotion of democracy and human rights.

At the same time, there are areas in which the interests of Russia or China may overlap with those of the United States and where cooperation on shared concerns is possible. China and Russia both express concerns over terrorism and its potential spillover effects.[65] As signatories of the JCPOA, China and Russia remain supportive, and China even played an important role in coaxing Iran to the table for negotiations.[66] China and the United States also maintain interest in stable oil markets. China is the world largest importer of oil, importing a substantial amount from the Middle East.[67]

Regional Conflicts and Aggression Strain World Order and Affect U.S. Security

Millions of people in the Middle East live their lives peacefully, untouched by violence or conflict. At the same time, the region is beset by a number of vicious conflicts that are degrading its ability to prosper or even ensure decent lives for many of its residents.

From a U.S. point of view, these conflicts can be divided into two types: those that involve a U.S. ally or partner and those that do not. The United States has a strong interest in the first type of conflict, including supporting its ally or partner and minimizing harm to that country. But the United

---

[65] Christine Wormuth, *Russia and China in the Middle East: Implications for the United States in an Era of Strategic Competition*, Testimony Presented Before the House Foreign Affairs Subcommittee on Middle East, North Africa and International Terrorism on May 9, 2019, Santa Monica, Calif.: RAND Corporation, CT-511, 2019.

[66] John W. Garver, *China and Iran: An Emerging Partnership Post-Sanctions*, Washington, D.C.: Middle East Institute, MEI Policy Focus 2016-3, February 2016; Mahmoudian and Cafiero, 2021.

[67] Alterman, 2020; Michael Singh, *China and the United States in the Middle East: Between Dependency and Rivalry*, Washington, D.C.: Washington Institute for Near East Policy, September 2020a.

States also has an interest in the second type. Conflicts can spill over; battle-trained terrorists can move across countries, resulting weak states provide vacuums that create space for proxy wars among regional actors; and conflicts can create destabilizing refugee flows, as occurred with the Syrian conflict. Countries at war have reduced trade and investment possibilities, lowering opportunity for prosperity for all. And conflicts run against long-standing global efforts to maintain a peaceful world order and prevent harm to people.

The United States has a long tradition of working with unrelated countries to end conflicts. President Rutherford B. Hayes in 1878 mediated a boundary dispute between Paraguay and Argentina stemming from a war between Paraguay and the triple alliance of Argentina, Brazil, and Uruguay. Likewise, President Theodore Roosevelt was awarded the Nobel Peace Prize in 1906 for negotiating peace in the 1904–1905 war between Russia and Japan. In more modern times, the United States played a leading role in ending conflicts in the Balkans in the 1990s and in mediating issues with Israel and the Palestinians.

Multiple conflicts fester in the Middle East, including three active civil wars in Syria, Yemen, and Libya. The Syria war, which started in 2011, has resulted in about 500,000 dead and 13 million people displaced either inside Syria or outside as refugees—over half the country's prewar population.[68] The Yemen war, which started in 2015, has killed more than 250,000 people, with an additional 150,000 children dying from starvation.[69] For the Libya civil war, it is difficult to find a count of all people killed; an estimated 400,000 had been displaced.[70] Libya's weak state institutions also enabled it to become one of the main transit points for "irregular" migrants (those arriving outside of established migration mechanisms) traveling from sub-Saharan Africa to the European Union.

---

[68] Phillip Connor, "Most Displaced Syrians are in the Middle East, and About a Million Are in Europe," *FactTank*, Pew Research Center, January 29, 2018; Carla E. Humud and Christopher M. Blanchard, *Armed Conflict in Syria: Overview and U.S. Response*, Washington, D.C.: Congressional Research Service, RL33487, July 27, 2020.

[69] Daniel Egel and Trevor Johnston, "Yemen's Chaos Creates a New Opportunity for the Biden-Harris Team," *The National Interest*, November 22, 2020.

[70] Christopher M. Blanchard, *Libya: Conflict, Transition, and U.S. Policy*, Washington, D.C.: Congressional Research Service, RL33142, June 26, 2020.

Each of these wars involves either the United States or U.S. allies and partners, sometimes on opposite sides. U.S. troops are present in Syria, largely to counter ISIS; troops from U.S. adversaries Russia and Iran and U.S. NATO ally Turkey are also present, and U.S. ally Israel conducts frequent air raids to counter Iran and its main proxy, Lebanese Hezbollah. In Yemen, a Saudi-led ten-member coalition fights against the Houthis, allied with Iran and considered an Iranian proxy group by some.[71] In Libya, NATO ally Turkey is supporting one side with arms, advisers, and Syrian proxy forces, while the United Arab Emirates, U.S. adversary Russia, Egypt, and Jordan are supporting the other side with arms, training, or private military contractors. In addition, NATO allies France and Italy are supporting different sides, through either training or other forms of support.[72]

There are other forms of aggression taking place in the Middle East. Iran supports a network of proxy groups, including Lebanese Hezbollah and militias in Iraq that present threats to U.S. allies and partners or to regional stability, along with the Houthis in Yemen. Hezbollah presents a threat to Israel, and the Iraqi militias are a destabilizing force as the central government tries to reform Iraq's economy and bring growth, and the Houthis lob missiles into Saudi Arabia. As part of this war, Saudi Arabia's use of U.S.-supplied weapons has killed numerous civilians, creating moral and ethical problems for the United States as it weighs the impacts of its arms sales; an early step of the Biden administration was a public review of this situation. Iran has also created instability by proliferating missiles, most

---

[71] Saudi Arabia and the United Arab Emirates actively conducted air strikes; Kuwait, Bahrain, Qatar, and Sudan contributed aircraft; Egypt contributed aircraft and naval vessels; the United States contributed logistical and intelligence support; and Jordan and Morocco offered unspecified support. In addition, Pakistan and Somalia said they supported the coalition (John Gambrell, "Here Are the Members of the Saudi-Led Coalition in Yemen and What They're Contributing," *Business Insider*, March 30, 2015). As of early 2021, Saudi Arabia was the main external participant in the civil war.

[72] Angus McDowell, "Factbox: Who's Involved in Libya's War and Why," Reuters, May 29, 2020.

predominantly to the Houthis, Hezbollah, and Hamas in the Gaza strip, and Iran's ballistic missiles threaten regional neighbors.[73]

The longest-running conflict in the region involves the United States' major non-NATO ally, Israel. Following the Israeli-Arab war of 1948, Israel signed armistice agreements with Egypt, Jordan, Lebanon, and Syria.[74] With peace agreements in 1979 between Israel and Egypt and in 1993 between Israel and Jordan, Israel is still technically at war with Iraq, Lebanon, and Syria, although no fighting is ongoing with those countries. Israel is also in conflict with some of the Palestinian Arab population, the Palestinian Authority of the West Bank, and Hamas in Gaza, with violence escalating most recently between Israel and Gaza in May 2021.

As noted at the beginning of this section, the United States has been a peacemaker since the nineteenth century. In 2020, the United States brokered normalization agreements between Israel and four Arab countries—Bahrain, Morocco, Sudan, and the United Arab Emirates—in a venture called the Abraham Accords.[75] The agreements have opened up financing opportunities for Arab-Israeli entrepreneurs and have given them an opportunity to integrate into the broader Middle East.[76] Those outcomes underscore the benefits of resolving conflicts as a core interest of the United States in the region. There were benefits beyond peace and economic interchange: although not overtly connected to the agreement, the United Arab Emirates gained the right to buy U.S. F-35 fighter jets; the United States removed

---

[73] For missiles to the Houthis, see Farzin Nadimi, "The UN Exposes Houthi Reliance on Iranian Weapons," Washington, D.C.: The Washington Institute for Near East Policy, Policy Watch 3261, February 13, 2020. For missiles to Hamas, see Adnan Abu Amer, "Hamas Opens Up on Arms, Missile Supplies from Iran," Al-Monitor, September 24, 2020. For missiles to Lebanese Hezbollah, see Shaan Shaikh, "Missiles and Rockets of Hezbollah," Missile Threat, Washington, D.C.: Center for Strategic and International Studies, June 26, 2018 (last modified September 27, 2019). For Iran's own program, see Michael Ellman, "Iran's Ballistic Missile Program," The Iran Primer, Washington, D.C.: U.S. Institute of Peace, January 13, 2021.

[74] For a brief history, see Office of the Historian, "The Arab-Israeli War of 1948," webpage, undated a. For armistice agreements, see United Nations, "Peace Agreements Database Search: Israel," 2019.

[75] U.S. Department of State, "The Abraham Accords," webpage, undated.

[76] Shira Rubin, "Long Sidelined, Arab Israeli Entrepreneurs Looking to Join Tech Boom with Emirati Backing," Washington Post, January 18, 2021.

Sudan from its list of state sponsors of terrorism; and the United States recognized Moroccan control over the disputed Western Sahara region.[77] In 2021, the United States facilitated an agreement to reduce tensions between Saudi Arabia and Qatar.[78]

Militarized Approaches Have Had High Human and Financial Costs

Addressing security risks in the Middle East has come at a high cost—both in terms of American lives and health and in terms of taxpayer dollars. Reducing the human and financial costs of U.S. policies and actions in the Middle East is important in its own right and can allow for greater investment in domestic needs and other pressing international concerns.

Ongoing conflicts in the greater Middle East have taken a heavy toll on the physical and mental health of a generation of Americans. Indeed, nearly all American military deaths—apart from training accidents—in the past four decades have been in the Middle East.[79] Since 2001, more than 1.9 million Americans have served more than 3 million tours of 30 days or longer as part of Operation Enduring Freedom (OEF) and Operation Iraqi Freedom (OIF).[80]

This has resulted in more than 7,000 deaths of U.S. service members[81] and at least 8,000 deaths of U.S. contractors (both U.S. and foreign

---

[77] Michael J. Koplow, "The Challenge of Solidifying the Abraham Accords," New York: Israel Policy Forum, January 7, 2021.

[78] Elena Moore, "Saudi Arabia and Qatar Lower Tensions in U.S.-Backed Agreement," NPR, January 5, 2021.

[79] Bacevich, 2016.

[80] Institute of Medicine (U.S.) Committee on the Initial Assessment of Readjustment Needs of Military Personnel, Veterans, and Their Families, "Operation Enduring Freedom and Operation Iraqi Freedom: Demographics and Impact," in *Returning Home from Iraq and Afghanistan: Preliminary Assessment of Readjustment Needs of Veterans, Service Members, and Their Families*, Washington, D.C.: National Academies Press, 2010.

[81] Defense Casualty Analysis System, "U.S. Military Casualties–OCO Casualty Summary by Casualty Type," table, Washington, D.C., March 2, 2021.

citizens).[82] While there is no complete public accounting of injuries, we can account for some key elements. Since 2000, more than 400,000 service members have experienced traumatic brain injuries.[83] While most recover quickly, 10–15 percent have enduring health consequences.[84] Wars have affected the mental health of service members.[85] Eleven to 20 percent of OEF/ OIF veterans have been diagnosed with post-traumatic stress disorder, while 13–15 percent have depressive symptoms. Eleven to 13 percent have substance use disorders, and another 12–40 percent have high-risk alcohol use.

In addition to costs associated with lost lives and damaged health of American veterans, war costs will burden American taxpayers for decades. There is no standardized, government-wide system dedicated to tracking war costs, and so estimates of total war-related expenditures vary based on different assumptions about which costs should be attributed to war. From 2001 to 2019, Congress appropriated $2 trillion to fund Department of Defense (DoD) activities designated either as emergency requirements or Overseas Contingency Operations, including the Global War on Terror.[86] These funds are not exclusively designated for operations in the Middle East and North Africa. By 2018, a total of $759 billion had been appropriated for obligations in Iraq.[87] Overseas Contingency Operations spending for

---

[82] Watson Institute for International and Public Affairs, "Costs of War: U.S. & Allied Killed," webpage, undated b.

[83] Military Health System, "Traumatic Brain Injury Center of Excellence," webpage, undated.

[84] Carrie M. Farmer, Heather Krull, Thomas W. Concannon, Molly M. Simmons, Francesca Pillemer, Teague Ruder, Andrew M. Parker, Maulik P. Purohit, Liisa Hiatt, Benjamin Saul Batorsky, and Kimberly A. Hepner, *Understanding Treatment of Mild Traumatic Brain Injury in the Military Health System*, Santa Monica, Calif.: RAND Corporation, RR-844-OSD, 2016.

[85] Eric R. Pedersen, Kathryn E. Bouskill, Stephanie Brooks Holliday, Jonathan Cantor, Sierra Smucker, Matthew L. Mizel, Lauren Skrabala, Aaron Kofner, Terri Tanielian, *Improving Substance Use Care: Addressing Barriers to Expanding Integrated Treatment Options for Post-9/11 Veterans*, Santa Monica, Calif.: RAND Corporation, RR-4354-WWP, 2020.

[86] Brendan W. McGarry and Emily M. Morgenstern, *Overseas Contingency Operations Funding: Background and Status*, Washington, D.C.: Congressional Research Service, R44519, September 6, 2019.

[87] Christopher T. Mann, *U.S. War Costs, Casualties, and Personnel Levels Since 9/11*, Washington, D.C.: Congressional Research Service, IF11182, April 18, 2019.

Iraq peaked in fiscal year (FY) 2008 with $140 billion obligated. However, between 2016 and 2019, U.S. spending dropped to an average of $11.3 billion per year on Operation Inherent Resolve in Iraq and Syria.[88] By way of comparison, over the same time frame, U.S. government spending averaged $4.1 trillion per year.[89]

These figures do not capture war-related expenditures in other U.S. government agencies. A frequently cited estimate from the Brown University Costs of War initiative is that the United States has spent $6.4 trillion on wars in Iraq, Syria, Afghanistan, and Pakistan.[90] This includes obligations for veterans, the State Department, the U.S. Agency for International Development (USAID), the Department of Homeland Security, and DoD. As the $6.4 trillion figure has been financed by borrowing, interest payments alone could cost an additional $2 trillion by 2030.[91]

Comparatively, spending on foreign assistance and security cooperation is paltry. From FY 2017 to FY 2021, DoD requested $820 million per year for security cooperation activities funded through the National Defense Strategy implementation account and in FY 2021 budgeted $7.5 billion for all security cooperation activities and programs worldwide.[92] In the past two decades, all foreign assistance to the Middle East amounted to only $198 billion—43 percent was designated as economic assistance, with the remainder for military assistance—but $100 billion of this was directed toward just three countries: Jordan, Egypt, and Israel.[93] This means that most other countries in the

---

[88] Average calculated from figures taken from the United States Department of Defense's Budget Request for fiscal years 2016–2019, Washington, D.C.: 2016–2019

[89] Average calculated from figures taken from the Congressional Budget Office's annual federal budget infographics, Washington, D.C.: 2016–2020.

[90] Watson Institute for International and Public Affairs, "Costs of War: Summary of Findings," webpage, undated a.

[91] Heidi Peltier, *The Cost of Debt-Financed War: Public Debt and Rising Interest for Post-9/11 War Spending*, Providence, R.I.: Brown University, Watson Institute for International & Public Affairs, January 2020.

[92] Office of the Secretary of Defense, *Fiscal Year (FY) 2021 President's Budget: Justification for Security Cooperation Program and Activity Funding*, Washington D.C., April 2020.

[93] Authors' calculations based on complete dataset from "Foreign Aid Explorer," https://foreignassistance.gov/.

Middle East receive comparatively little such investment. Increases in diplomatic and economic foreign assistance efforts relative to military efforts have been a notable request from the defense establishment for years.[94]

Civilian Displacement Is Harmful and Destabilizing

The Middle East has a greater proportion of its population displaced—internally within a state or as refugees who have fled to another country—than any other region of the world. Altogether, there are 20.5 million forcibly displaced people in or from the Middle East and North Africa (MENA) region,[95] out of a population of 450 million.[96] That is nearly 5 percent of the region's population. Displacement is a result of ongoing unresolved conflicts and weak states that are unable to maintain security. Syria is the biggest contributor, with over half of its total population displaced. The Palestinian refugee population dates back over 70 years. Wars in Iraq and Yemen and the failed Libyan state also contribute. In recent decades, the United States has even used its military power to stem refugee flows in the Middle East, such as implementing the Northern No-Fly Zone to protect 1.85 million refugees in the Kurdistan Region of Iraq from the Saddam Hussein Regime (enabling most of them to return home quickly) and using air power to protect thousands of Yazidis in Iraq from displacement and mass slaughter by ISIS.[97] These devastating humanitarian situations pose a number of security and economic risks to the United States and its allies in the Middle East and Europe.

First, there is no plan underway for durable solutions for displaced populations in the Middle East, apart from ongoing humanitarian aid. For most, there is no end to their displacement in sight, with few active diplomatic efforts to end conflicts as a prerequisite for returning. Middle East host

---

[94] Robert M. Gates, "The Overmilitarization of American Foreign Policy," *Foreign Affairs*, July/August 2020.

[95] United Nations High Commissioner for Refugees (UNHCR), *Global Trends: Forced Displacement in 2019*, Copenhagen, Denmark, June 18, 2020.

[96] World Bank, "Population, Total—Middle East & North Africa," webpage, undated b.

[97] Peter W. Galbraith, "Refugees from War in Iraq: What Happened in 1991 and What May Happen in 2003," Migration Policy Institute, No. 2, February, 2003; The White House, "Statement by the President," August 7, 2014.

countries do not allow their displaced populations to fully integrate. For instance, many Palestinians in Lebanon and Jordan still live in camps and have limited right to work. Resettlement countries globally have reduced numbers that they are taking. With the exception of the past few years, the United States is the country taking the most refugees for resettlement, taking 62 percent of all resettled refugees in 2015.[98] While President Biden committed to raising resettlement numbers to 62,500 in 2021 and 125,000 in 2022,[99] this is a mere drop in the bucket of the global displaced population of 80 million. Not having prospects for return, integration, or moving on presents problems for the displaced people involved, for their host communities and countries, and for the stability for the world. The existence of a regional underclass living in insecurity, with low access to education and jobs, and the strains that these place on their host communities pose a chronic risk of instability.[100]

Second, large numbers of people living in displacement may create space for future radicalization and militarization. The Middle East has a history of conflict involving its refugee populations, such as civil wars in Jordan and Lebanon. History shows examples of refugee populations that have become radicalized; these have often been communities with lower access to opportunities, such as education and jobs, than their host communities.[101]

Third, migration flows out of the Middle East have been a destabilizing factor for the European Union. From 2009 to 2018, 3.4 million irregular

---

[98] UNHCR, "Resettlement Data Finder (RDF)," webpage, undated b.

[99] Abigail Hauslohner, "Biden Seeks to Restore 'Badly Damaged' Refugee Resettlement Program," *Washington Post*, February 5, 2021.

[100] Shelly Culbertson and Louay Constant, *Education of Syrian Refugee Children: Managing the Crisis in Turkey, Lebanon, and Jordan*, Santa Monica, Calif.: RAND Corporation, RR-859-CMEPP, 2015; Krishna B. Kumar, Shelly Culbertson, Louay Constant, Shanthi Nataraj, Fatih Unlu, Kathryn E. Bouskill, Joy S. Moini, Katherine Costello, Gursel Rafig oglu Aliyev, and Fadia Afashe, *Opportunities for All: Mutually Beneficial Opportunities for Syrians and Host Countries in Middle Eastern Labor Markets*, Santa Monica, Calif.: RAND Corporation, RR-2653-QFFD, 2018.

[101] Barbara Sude, David Stebbins, and Sarah Weilant, *Lessening the Risk of Refugee Radicalization: Lessons for the Middle East from Past Crises*, Santa Monica, Calif.: RAND Corporation, PE-166-OSD, 2015.

migrants (traveling outside of established immigration channels) from the Middle East (such as from Syria and Iraq) and sub-Saharan Africa arrived in the European Union.[102] Numbers peaked at 1.8 million in 2015. The migration surges led to a general backlash and rise in support for right-wing and populist political parties that opposed their countries' continued participation in the European Union and NATO—the basis for the post–World War II European security order. In response, the European Union took measures to strengthen its borders and collaborate with transit countries (such as Turkey and Libya) to reduce migration. However, the migration pressures remain, and another destabilizing migration surge into Europe remains a possibility.

Fourth, the United States is the most significant global funder helping refugees. It is the largest donor to the UN High Commissioner for Refugees (UNHCR), larger than the next nine countries combined.[103] Yet in recent years, while the United States provided humanitarian assistance, it has not taken a large role in resolving conflicts or finding solutions, and few other countries are in a position to do so. The United States is therefore funding support for an ever-growing population of displaced people. These growing numbers and the lack of solutions to the problems related to displacement challenge both American humanitarian values and others' confidence in the American role as a problem-solver.

Climate Change Impacts Exacerbate Other Security Challenges

Climate change may serve as a threat multiplier for a range of other risks in the Middle East in several ways, including by interacting with energy security, economic stability, state fragility, food and water scarcity, and mass migration. The Biden administration has deemed climate change as among its top priorities. President Biden stated that climate change is "an essential

---

[102] Charles Ries and Shelly Culbertson, "This Is How Europe Dealt with Migration," *The National Interest*, December 1, 2018.

[103] UNHCR, "Government Partners," webpage, undated a.

element of U.S. foreign policy and national security."[104] Climate was acknowledged as a security consideration by DoD in its 2010 Quadrennial Defense Review Report and will be included in the next National Defense Strategy.[105] This effort to address climate change may spur a more rapid transition away from fossil fuels, which could upset the social contracts and economies of oil exporters. However, as noted above, this is a slow-moving trend that is unlikely to have a sizable effect for decades.

The Middle East is the hottest and most water-poor region in the world and is projected to be one of the most affected by climate change.[106] This will strain livelihoods, governance, and habitability in parts of the region.[107] Temperatures are projected to rise more quickly than the global average; by the end of the century, up to 200 days annually may register at 122 degrees Fahrenheit.[108] Freshwater shortages may become prevalent. For instance, precipitation levels may fall by 40 percent in North Africa by 2100.[109]

Climate change may undermine regional security through the loss of livelihood from depletion of water and loss of arable land. In Syria, starting in 2006, the most severe drought in a century cost 800,000 Syrians their livelihoods in four years and led 1.5 million people to migrate to cities. Some

---

[104] Somini Sengupta, "How Biden's Climate Ambitions Could Shift America's Global Footprint," *New York Times*, January 27, 2021.

[105] DoD, *Quadrennial Defense Review Report*, Washington, D.C., February 2010; Tony Bertuca, "Austin Pledges to Include Climate Change Review in Upcoming National Defense Strategy," *Inside Defense*, January 27, 2021.

[106] Peter Schwartzstein, "The Perfect Storm: Coronavirus and Climate Change in the Middle East," Project on Middle East Democracy, April 3, 2020.

[107] Jeremy S. Pal and Elfatih A. B. Eltahir, "Future Temperature in Southwest Asia Projected to Exceed a Threshold for Human Adaptability," *Nature Climate Change*, Vol. 6, 2016, pp. 197–200; Caitlin E. Werrell and Fancesco Femia, "Fragile States: The Nexus of Climate Change, State Fragility and Migration," *ANGLE Journal*, November 24, 2015.

[108] Johannes Lelieveld and Panos Hadjinicolaou, "Climate-Exodus Expected in the Middle East and North Africa," Max-Planck-Gesellschaft, May 2, 2016; Jos Lelieveld, Yiannis Proestos, Panos Hadjinicolaou, Meryem Tanarhte, Evangelos Tyrlis, and Georgios Zittis, "Strongly Increasing Heat Extremes in the Middle East and North Africa (MENA) in the 21st Century," *Climatic Change*, Vol. 137, 2016, pp. 245–260.

[109] Regional Bureau for Arab States, *Water Governance in the Arab Region: Managing Scarcity and Securing the Future*, New York: United Nations Development Programme, 2013.

attribute mass migration and unemployment as a contributing factor to the protests that later devolved into Syria's civil war.[110] With the Tigris and the Euphrates possibly running dry by the end of the century, Iraq faces similar economic risks. Some countries that depend on desalinization (such as in the Gulf) will require new technologies to outpace rising salinity levels associated with climate change.[111] Mass migration as a result of loss of livelihoods from climate change may become more common, destabilizing some countries.[112]

Environmental collapses and their economic fallout have been seized upon by armed groups in recruitment.[113] After Somalia's ruinous drought and desertification in 2016 and 2017, observers noted an uptick in the recruitment activities of ISIS and Al-Shabaab.

Competition for water resources can increase geopolitical tensions. Control over the Jordan River has been a point of contention for years between Jordan and Israel.[114] Tensions are ongoing between Egypt and Ethiopia over Ethiopia's plans to build the Grand Ethiopian Renaissance Dam, and Turkish and Iranian dams have caused friction with Iraq.[115]

At the same time, a focus on climate change through a security lens offers some opportunities. The Abraham Accords paved the way for sharing of water desalination technology from Israel to Bahrain, Qatar, and potentially other countries in the region that have overexploited their water resources. Iran's government recognizes climate change as a security issue, as the country suffers from dwindling water supplies, extreme

---

[110] Colin P. Kelley, Shahrzad Mohtadi, Mark A. Cane, Richard Seager, and Yochanan Kushnir, "Climate Change in the Fertile Crescent and Implications of the Recent Syrian Drought," *Proceedings of the National Academy of Sciences*, Vol. 112, 2015, pp. 3241–3246.

[111] José Edson, Ilana Wainer, and Bruno Ferrero, *Final Technical: Regional Desalination and Climate Change*, Abu Dhabi: Abu Dhabi Global Environmental Data Initiative, 2016.

[112] Werrell and Femia, 2015.

[113] Peter Schwartzstein, "Climate Change and Water Woes Drove ISIS Recruiting in Iraq," *National Geographic*, November 14, 2017.

[114] Erika Weinthal and Neda Zawahri, "Don't Politicize Water," *Foreign Policy*, September 17, 2020.

[115] "Climate Change Is Making the Arab World More Miserable," *The Economist*, June 2, 2018.

drought, and desertification.[116] Sanctions have prevented it from building improved infrastructure to address some of these problems. Addressing climate risks could be one area where the United States and Iran could find common ground amid otherwise tense relations and negotiations.

The United States Benefits from the Well-being of Its Allies and Partners

The United States has a dense web of allies and partners in the Middle East, in both security and economics. U.S. reliance on and praise of allies and partners is long-term and bipartisan. The Trump administration's 2017 National Security Strategy noted that "allies and partners magnify our power," although it also said that "we expect them to shoulder a fair share of the burden of responsibility to protect against common threats."[117] In his first major foreign policy address as president, President Biden said, "America's alliances are our greatest asset, and leading with diplomacy means standing shoulder-to-shoulder with our allies and key partners once again."[118]

In the realm of security, the region has one NATO ally: Turkey; seven out of the United States's formally designated 17 major non-NATO allies: Bahrain, Egypt, Israel, Jordan, Kuwait, Morocco, and Tunisia; and two "major security partners": Bahrain and the United Arab Emirates.[119] In addition,

---

[116] Mana Mostatabi, "Sanctioning Iran's Climate," *MENASource*, May 1, 2019.

[117] The White House, *National Security Strategy of the United States of America*, Washington, D.C., December 2017, p. 4.

[118] The White House, "Remarks by President Biden on America's Place in the World," Washington, D.C., February 4, 2021.

[119] "Major non-NATO ally" is a statutory designation that allows designated countries to receive certain defense benefits. In addition to 17 designated major non-NATO allies, Taiwan is treated as such an ally, but without the designation (U.S. Department of State, "Major Non-NATO Ally Status," Fact Sheet, Washington, D.C.: Bureau of Political-Military Affairs, January 20, 2021). "Major security partner" was a designation created toward the end of the Trump administration and applies only to Bahrain and the United Arab Emirates, the two original Arab signatories to the Abraham Accords normalization agreements with Israel (The White House, "Statement from the Press Secretary Regarding the Designations of the UAE and Kingdom of Bahrain as Major Security Partners of the United States," Washington, D.C., January 15, 2021).

the U.S. military has some kind of presence, such as an air base, a naval base, or a smaller military facility, in at least 12 countries in the region.[120] Beyond major agreements and physical presence, there are numerous other smaller security agreements as well as training and arms sales. In addition, formal arrangements may not fully reflect security partnerships. Although not a designated major non-NATO ally nor a signatory to a formal mutual defense treaty, Saudi Arabia has long been an important if difficult U.S. security partner in the region.[121] Notably, it is the largest purchaser of U.S. arms through the foreign military sales program.[122]

In the economic realm, the United States has free trade agreements with five countries in the Middle East: Bahrain, Israel, Jordan, Morocco, and Oman, out of 20 countries globally.[123] It has bilateral investment treaties, which provide for investor rights and protections, with Bahrain, Egypt, Jordan, Morocco, Tunisia, and Turkey.[124] A final type of agreement is the trade and investment framework agreement, which sets out principles for dialogue on issues of international economic exchange. The United States has such agreements with every Middle Eastern country except Iran and Syria.[125]

---

[120] The American Security Project lists facilities or bases in U.S. countries of interest in an interactive map updated February 9, 2021, and based originally on a 2018 publication. These include Bahrain, Egypt, Iraq, Israel, Jordan, Kuwait, Oman, Qatar, Saudi Arabia, Turkey, and the United Arab Emirates. Also listed is a base in Djibouti (Matthew Wallin, *U.S. Military Bases and Facilities in the Middle East*, Fact Sheet, American Security Project, June 2018; and American Security Project, "U.S. Bases in the Middle East," interactive map, February 9, 2021). In addition, the United States had a base or smaller military outpost in Tunisia and Libya as of the beginning of 2019 (Stephanie Savell and 5W Infographics, "This Map Shows Where in the World the U.S. Military is Combatting Terrorism," *Smithsonian Magazine*, January/February 2019).

[121] Robert D. Blackwill, *Trump's Foreign Policies Are Better Than They Seem*, Council Special Report No. 84, Washington, D.C.: Council on Foreign Relations, April 2019, pp. 44–46.

[122] U.S. Department of State, "U.S. Relations with Saudi Arabia," Bilateral Relations Fact Sheet, Washington, D.C.: Bureau of Near Eastern Affairs, December 15, 2020.

[123] U.S. Trade Representative, "Free Trade Agreements," webpage, undated a.

[124] As of early 2021, the United States had 42 such agreements. U.S. Department of Commerce, Office of Trade Agreements Negotiation and Compliance, "Bilateral Investment Treaties," webpage, undated.

[125] U.S. Trade Representative, "Trade and Investment Framework Agreements," webpage, undated c.

Allies and partners can magnify U.S. power by hosting bases; serving as partners in military operations, such as those conducted by the Syrian Democratic Forces against ISIS; adding legitimacy to a foreign-policy initiative; sharing intelligence; and numerous other activities that support U.S. national security.

But alliances and partnerships also have costs. First, they oblige the United States to spend resources and possibly lives in defense of other countries. The 2017 National Security Strategy raised this issue when it said that Iranian ballistic missile development threatens not just the United States, but allies as well, and that the United States is applying its efforts to prevent terrorist attacks on allies and partners.[126] Another cost is the risk of getting drawn into conflicts that do not serve U.S. interests. The Yemen war serves as one example. The United States supported a Saudi-led coalition comprised of ten countries established in 2015 to conduct military operations in Yemen against the Iran-supported Houthi movement.[127] Although an element of the U.S. and regional effort against Iran, the war also evolved into a humanitarian disaster and a site of alleged war crimes, with some contending that the United States could be held responsible.[128] In early February 2021, the Biden administration reduced support for some operations in Yemen and appointed a special envoy to work toward a diplomatic solution.[129]

U.S. credibility as an alliance partner is a factor in the extent to which allies will support U.S. goals.[130] For example, when the United States halted

---

[126] The White House, 2017, p. 26.

[127] Jeremy M. Sharp, Christopher M. Blanchard, and Sarah R. Collins, *Congress and the War in Yemen: Oversight and Legislation 2015–2020*, Washington, D.C.: Congressional Research Service, R45046, June 19, 2020; and U.S. Department of State, "U.S. Relations with Yemen," Bilateral Relations Fact Sheet, Washington, D.C.: Bureau of Near Eastern Affairs, December 30, 2020.

[128] Human Rights Watch, "Yemen: Events of 2020," webpage, undated.

[129] The White House, 2021; Warren P. Strobel, "Biden Launches Fresh Effort to End Civil War in Yemen, Halting 'Offensive' Aid to Saudis, Naming Envoy," *Wall Street Journal*, February 4, 2021.

[130] Natan Sachs, "Whose Side Are You On? Alliance Credibility in the Middle East and Japan," *Order from Chaos*, May 31, 2016; Michael Doran, "Obama's Secret Iran Strategy," *Mosaic Magazine*, February 2, 2015.

military aid to Egypt following the coup against elected leader Mohammed Morsi, Egypt signed a $3.5 billion arms deal with Russia.[131] At the same time, as the most powerful and richest nation on earth, the United States also has leverage.[132] There is no formula for alliance management, but essential elements include recognition that neither side benefits by dictating conditions of cooperation.

Societal Dysfunction Leads to Chronic Instability with Worldwide Repercussions

Many governments in the Middle East fall short in meeting the needs of their societies, and in particular in meeting the needs of their youth. Protests led to government overthrows in four countries, civil wars in Syria, Libya, and Yemen, and moderate changes in others. Follow-on waves of protests from 2018 to 2021 in 12 countries have been dubbed "Arab Spring 2.0."[133] This desire for change is most recently exemplified by mass protests in 2019 in Iraq, where people kept returning to the streets despite coming under fire from armed groups—some formally connected to the state—that killed more than 500 and wounded more than 19,000.[134] The Arab Spring protests were collective expressions of frustration with two main issues: lack of economic opportunity and problems of governance—in particular corruption.[135] As problems of chronic instability in the Middle East spill over to the rest of the

---

[131] James Sladden, Becca Wasser, Ben Connable, and Sarah Grand-Clement, *Russian Strategy in the Middle East*, Santa Monica, Calif.: RAND Corporation, PE-236-RC, 2017.

[132] Ariane M. Tabatabai and Becca Wasser, "Could America Use Its Leverage to Alter the Saudis' Behavior?" *Newsweek*, November 15, 2018.

[133] Marwan Muasher, "Is This the Arab Spring 2.0?" Washington, D.C.: Carnegie Endowment for International Peace, October 30, 2019.

[134] Renad Mansour, Thanassis Cambanis, and Michael Wahid Hanna, "These Iraqi Militias Are Attacking Protesters and Getting Away with It. Here's Why," *Washington Post*, November 18, 2019; Alissa J. Rubin, "Iraq in Worst Political Crisis in Years as Death Toll Mounts from Protests," *New York Times*, December 21, 2019.

[135] Elena Ianchovichina, *Eruptions of Popular Anger: The Economics of the Arab Spring and Its Aftermath*, Washington, D.C.: International Bank for Reconstruction and Development, The World Bank, 2018.

world, our hypothesis is that American security interests in the Middle East are inherently tied to improved economic opportunities and more accountable governance in the region.

Economies in the region continue to fail to produce enough jobs for young people. The Middle East and North Africa have had the highest youth unemployment rates in the world for over 25 years, ranging between 25 percent and 30 percent since the 1990s.[136] The Middle East is not harnessing this pool of talent. The Middle East's youth bulge in combination with low economic growth exacerbates these challenges. Half of the population of the MENA region is under the age of 24, and the regional population is expected to double in the first half of this century.[137] While countries range from the richest in the world to the poorest, GDP growth across the region is tepid, averaging only 0.47 percent in 2019.[138] Moreover, education systems are poor, not providing graduates with the skills they need.[139] Many young people in the Middle East therefore spend years between finishing school and starting employment in "waithood," a period of limbo between childhood and adulthood.[140] The literature links high youth unemployment with political instability.[141]

---

[136] Nader Kabbani, *Youth Employment in the Middle East and North Africa: Revisiting and Reframing the Challenge*, Washington, D.C.: The Brookings Institution, February 26, 2019.

[137] Veera Mendonca, Momo Duehring, Arthur van Diesen, Jan Beise, Sinae Lee, Bin Lian, Anastasia Mshvidobadze, and Danzhen You, *MENA Generation 2030: Investing in Children and Youth Today to Secure a Prosperous Region Tomorrow*, UNICEF, Division of Data, Research, and Policy, April 2019.

[138] World Bank, "GDP Growth (Annual %)–Middle East & North Africa," webpage, undated a.

[139] United Nations Children's Fund (UNICEF), Middle East and North Africa, "Education Response to COVID-19," webpage, undated.

[140] Caroline Krafft and Ragui Assaad, "Employment's Role in Enabling and Constraining Marriage in the Middle East and North Africa," *Demography*, Vol. 57, No. 6, 2020, pp. 2297–2325; Diane Singerman, *The Economic Imperatives of Marriage: Emerging Practices and Identities Among Youth in the Middle East*, Dubai, UAE: Wolfensohn Center for Development, Dubai School of Government, Middle East Youth Initiative Working Paper No. 6, September 2007.

[141] Therese F. Azeng and Thierry U. Yogo, *Youth Unemployment and Political Instability in Selected Developing Countries*, Belvédère, Tunisia: African Development Bank,

Problems with governance are many in the Middle East; they include lack of accountability, authoritarianism, human rights violations, and poor quality public services. Corruption in particular has fed public frustration and the region's protests. A 2019 Transparency International survey found that the police forces in the Middle East are the institutions most likely to ask for and receive bribes.[142] Sixty-five percent thought corruption was on the rise. At the same time, the survey noted bright spots, as the United Arab Emirates, Qatar, and Israel ranked relatively high globally; and people in Bahrain, Saudi Arabia, Libya, and Iraq thought that corruption had declined slightly.

Some governments have sought improvements in response, including shifting their policies toward governance reform and job creation. This is especially true in the Gulf as governments contemplate rising populations and the potential longer-term decline in the global use of hydrocarbons; Saudi Arabia's Vision 2030 document encapsulates this trend.[143] Tunisia, while struggling economically, developed a new constitution blending both Islamic and Western ideals and governs with a unity government that unites Islamist and secular parties.

Yet, overall the problems are not improving. Chronic instability, shrinking economies, and views that corruption are on the rise indicate that the reasons for the protests have not abated. While there has been no shortage of research or advice, regional governments cannot or will not take needed steps to address corruption and improve their economies.[144]

The general frustration with stagnant economies and unaccountable governments is posing risks to the regional order. Competing visions of a new regional order in the Middle East are emerging, both by youthful protesters wanting better jobs and more accountability and by violent extremist

---

Group Working Paper Series No. 171, May 2013; Aniruddha Bagchi and Jomon Paul, "Youth Unemployment and Terrorism in the MENAP (Middle East, North Africa, Afghanistan, and Pakistan) Region," *Socio-Economic Planning Sciences*, Vol. 64, December 2018, pp. 9–20; and Henrik Urdal, "A Clash of Generations? Youth Bulges and Political Violence," *International Studies Quarterly*, Vol. 50, 2006, pp. 607–629.

[142] Transparency International, "What People Think: Corruption in the Middle East and North Africa," December 11, 2019.

[143] Kingdom of Saudi Arabia, *Saudi Vision 2030*, Riyadh, 2016.

[144] Kabbani, 2019.

groups that reject the existence of the nation-state system in the Middle East and call for a caliphate instead. Henry Kissinger described "an imploding regional order" in the Middle East with challenges to the very legitimacy and effectiveness of the nation-state.[145] And despite the pitfalls, a majority of Middle East populations views the Arab Spring positively.[146] As turmoil in the Middle East has consistently spilled over into security threats for the United States, it is in U.S. security interests to help address the causes of such turmoil and support countries in improving accountability and economic opportunities. The United States to date has not made efforts toward improving economies and government accountability in the Middle East commensurate with its military activity in the region.

---

[145] Henry Kissinger, *World Order*, London: Penguin, 2015, p. 128.

[146] Arab Center Washington D.C., 2020.

CHAPTER 3

Conclusions and Recommendations

U.S. interests remain embedded in the Middle East. The Middle East sits at the crossroads of many issues that affect American national security. There is no reason to assume that quiet will prevail in the region during the next four or eight years and enable the United States to turn its back, deprioritize it, and withdraw attention. Therefore, it is in the United States' best interest to recognize its full range of security interests and proactively manage them.

However, keeping the region a priority does not mean keeping the status quo of military presence or other approaches. Rather, in light of the changed context in the United States, including the pandemic and the focus on great power competition, and the changed context in the Middle East as described here, renewed strategic effort is called for to find new ways to manage U.S. interests. This can best be done by modifying the U.S. balance of use of military tools and civilian tools, both because diplomatic, economic, and technical assistance tools are better suited to certain issues and because the United States is seeking to free up military assets for Asia.

A bottom-line aspiration would be for the Middle East to be a "normal" region. Being a normal region means meeting the positive aspirations of the region's citizens, with states having capacity to maintain security and stability within their borders, provide quality public services for their citizens, and build prosperity and better opportunities through strong economies and trade. Ideally, the Middle East would become a region where civil wars are not ongoing, threats are not emanating, U.S. military engagements are not occurring, large numbers of people are not displaced, great and regional powers do not engage in proxy wars, people are not drawn to participate in violent extremism, American lives are not at risk, American taxpayer dollars are not consumed at the rates they have been in recent decades, and neighboring countries do not compete with each other to produce weapons of mass destruction.

In light of these aspirations and significant changes in the United States and the Middle East, we offer a set of recommendations meant to provide options to pursue these goals, manage U.S. security interests in the Middle East, rebalance tools to reduce reliance on the military, proactively mitigate risk, maintain successes, de-escalate conflict, and remain engaged in the region to better respond to the inevitable new events on the ground rather than be caught off guard. Some of these recommendations are new because of this changed context, while others may be newly possible because of these changes. At the same time, each of these recommendations has risks, constraints, and trade-offs, and not all can be done at once. Yet despite the constraints, we view these as worth the risks and newly possible due to the changes described here in the United States and Middle East. Some of the recommendations are mutually reinforcing, with certain steps making others easier. Table 3.1 summarizes the recommendations and the U.S. security interests that they address.

The United States has a broad range of tools for carrying out these recommendations well beyond the military tool that has been prominent in relations with the Middle East for decades. These include efforts to advance trade and investment and assist with private-sector development and social development through aid and other means. Educational and cultural exchanges, greater opportunities for education and training in the United States, and stronger messaging about U.S. goals and activities can help the region and the United States meet their priorities. Diplomacy will necessarily play an important role in building bilateral and regional relations, along with dealing with outside powers in the region in a constructive manner.

TABLE 3.1

Recommendations and the U.S. Security Interests Addressed

Recommendation	What Is Different? What Unmet Needs Does This Address? What Are the Constraints?	Security Interests Addressed
Develop a U.S. interagency Middle East strategy that keeps the region as a priority while relying more on civilian tools • Define interests and goals • Align civilian and military activities • Rebalance tools to reduce reliance on military • Communicate intentions	• There is no public U.S. Middle East strategy that links objectives with tools and coordinates activities of U.S. agencies toward common goals. • The United States has relied heavily on military tools in the Middle East, and should shift more to civilian tools. • Changing U.S. policies have made the U.S. government look inconsistent and unreliable to some allies and partners. • The American public believes the Middle East is important to its security. A strategy would communicate to them what the plan is. • *Constraints*: Friendly nations could react adversely to deprioritization of their issues, while hostile nations could use information to undermine U.S. plans.	• All security interests
Develop substitute approaches to manage risks when reducing the U.S. military footprint in the Middle East • Align force posture with the Middle East strategy, making changes and cutting costs while meeting security goals • Increase security cooperation, in alignment with the Middle East strategy • Reconsider the weight of military assistance to key countries	• Many are calling to deprioritize the Middle East in comparison with other regions, reduce the U.S. footprint there to focus on great power competition with China, and cut costs. Changes should both meet security goals described in this report and increase cost-effectiveness. • The United States should not disengage to an extent that partners and allies increasingly rely on China and Russia instead of the United States for their arms and security cooperation. • U.S. force posture and security cooperation have not been fully in line with strategic goals, with effectiveness clearly measurable. • The United States relies increasingly on partners to manage security in the Middle East. Yet it invests relatively little in partner capacity building, and mechanisms to understand and improve effectiveness are underdeveloped. Therefore, security cooperation should receive greater targeted investment so partners they have the needed capabilities.	• All security interests

Table 3.1—Continued

Recommendation	What Is Different? What Unmet Needs Does This Address? What Are the Constraints?	Security Interests Addressed
Maintain an integrated, long-term strategy with Iran • Include the wide range of security interests • Take a containment and de-escalation approach, supporting partners • Collaborate on mutual interests with Iran • Embark on efforts to calm, if not end, the Iran-Saudi rivalry	• Security cooperation in the past focused mostly on terrorism. Additional targets should be strengthening internal security and missile defenses, so partners are not so vulnerable to Iranian backed militias and ballistic missiles. • JCPOA addressed only nuclear issues. Now that it is being revisited, it is important to keep the wider range of Iranian activities, particularly ballistic missiles and support for proxies, in mind. • Expand the pie to include common interests. • Support weak states (particularly Iraq and Lebanon) in dominating security within their borders to counter Iran's backing of militias. • U.S. policy has focused on Iran's nuclear proliferation, neglecting the Saudi-Iran tensions that are destabilizing in multiple countries. • *Constraints:* Iran may choose to not cooperate with U.S. initiatives, and when power rotates among U.S. parties, U.S. approaches may change quickly.	• Nuclear nonproliferation • Regional conflicts • Well-being of allies and partners • Climate change impacts
Mediate the end of conflicts and broker pragmatic solutions to civilian displacement • Focus on resolving one conflict first • Create a plan for durable solutions for all Middle East displaced people in ten years	• In recent years, the United States has focused its conflict-resolution efforts on defeating ISIS in Iraq and Syria and mediating the Abraham Accords, with success in both, yet efforts to broker agreements on civil wars in Syria, Yemen, and Libya have so far failed or lacked persistent diplomatic attention. • There is no effort to find durable solutions for Middle East refugees over the next ten years, and there are no out-of-the-box approaches such as expanded work visas.	• Terrorism • Great power competition • Regional conflicts • Forced displacement • Well-being of allies and partners • Rule of law and opportunities

Table 3.1—Continued

Recommendation	What Is Different? What Unmet Needs Does This Address? What Are the Constraints?	Security Interests Addressed
Focus U.S. development assistance on addressing two main causes of Arab Spring protests • Invest particularly in jobs (education and job creation) and rule of law (police corruption)	• *Constraints:* Conflict resolution in some cases may require collaborating with violent regimes or leaders, which would create ethical and moral quandaries for the United States. Parties to the conflicts may not work collaboratively. Iran or other entities may act to undermine efforts. Political will to take steps toward durable solutions may be lacking in countries of origin, refugee host countries, and resettlement countries. • U.S. foreign assistance addresses many issues, but is not specifically focused to the extent needed on jobs and corruption. • These issues are not improving on their own in the Middle East. • Neither the 2018 National Security Strategy nor the 2021 Interim Guidance mention these two issues as targets. • Middle East countries neglect career and technical education. • *Constraints:* Governments could view U.S. approaches as a violation of their sovereignty. Some could find the Chinese model of economic growth, with state-led economies and strict policing, more appealing. Economic reforms needed for job creation are not simple, even for motivated governments.	• Terrorism • Human and financial costs • Well-being of allies and partners • Rule of law and opportunities
Improve trust in the United States as a strong, consistent, reliable partner of choice • Apply consistent policies over time • Meet American security interests and values	• U.S. policies have been viewed as inconsistent, and this has reduced its ability to solve problems and put its long-term status as partner of choice in the Middle East at risk. • *Constraints:* Each administration has the ability and democratic mandate to change its foreign policy approaches.	• Energy markets • Great power competition • Lower human and financial costs to manage our interests

51

Table 3.1—Continued

Recommendation	What Is Different? What Unmet Needs Does This Address? What Are the Constraints?	Security Interests Addressed
Maintain an integrated program for countering violent extremism • Coordinate tools from multiple U.S. agencies • Understand radicalization processes • Continue targeted military efforts • Find solutions for ISIS fighters and families	• While an interagency strategy was developed in 2016, it was not implemented, and approaches remained mainly militarized. • The evidence base on the radicalization process, as well as effective deradicalization approaches, is weak and remains a gap. • ISIS fighters, ISIS wives, and their children remain in detention in northern Syria. There is no multilateral process to develop solutions. • Constraints: Terrorist groups will likely never be eradicated by any approaches; management of terrorist threats will be a long-term need.	• Terrorism • Human and financial costs • Well-being of allies and partners • Rule of law and opportunities
Facilitate regional interactions, mutual assistance, and security dialogues • Revive U.S. efforts to establish security forum • Use forum to resolve civil wars and tensions	• The Middle East is the only region without a function forum for security dialogue and cooperation. • The Middle East Strategic Alliance (MESA) was not started because of disagreements about scope. • A forum could also involve Israel, Turkey, and Iran. • Constraints: Many previous attempts to establish such a forum have not succeeded because of regional tensions and disagreements about scope. Some countries will not be interested in participation.	• All security interests
Invest in encouraging the linchpin countries of Iraq and Tunisia on the path to success—Iraq and Tunisia • Ensure the Middle East has examples of postwar and post–Arab Spring prosperity	• Iraq struggles with economic reform, implementing accountability, and vulnerability to Iranian-backed militias. • While Tunisia implemented Arab Spring reforms, its economy struggles. • Constraints: Both Iraq and Tunisia have some level of dysfunctional political tensions, and corruption and other issues distort their economies.	• All security interests

Develop a U.S. Interagency Middle East Strategy That Keeps the Region as a Priority While Relying More on Civilian Tools

The context in both the United States and in the Middle East has changed. This calls for redefining U.S. security strategy to adapt to new or evolving challenges, take advantage of new opportunities, reduce reliance on the U.S. military, and shift toward greater emphasis on diplomacy and other civilian tools.[1] Indeed, a 2019 Pew survey found that a majority of both Democrats and Republicans viewed diplomacy as more important than military strength in ensuring peace.[2]

The United States has not published a specific strategy for the Middle East. In contrast, the United States has had a well-developed strategy for the Indo-Pacific region, first introduced at the classified level in 2017 and then publicly released in early 2021.[3] While the 2018 National Defense Strategy contains a regional discussion about the Middle East, it takes the form of a brief set of high-level principles. The 2021 Interim National Security Strategic Guidance contains a paragraph of high-level principles and a reference to changing military presence.[4]

Therefore, our first recommendation is for the U.S. government to develop and publicly articulate an interagency strategy for the Middle East. There could of course be different levels of detail in a public version and a classified version. The strategy should define U.S. interests and goals, integrate and align civilian and military activities with the goals, and increase reliance on civilian agencies when appropriate. It should also draw on U.S. alliances to meet the stated objectives and to define roles for partners to collaborate and share responsibilities. This effort may produce a more

---

[1] For additional discussion of relying more on civilian tools in the Middle East, see Dalia Dassa Kaye, Linda Robinson, Jeffrey Martini, Nathan Vest, and Ashley L. Rhoades, *Reimagining U.S. Strategy in the Middle East: Sustainable Partnerships, Strategic Investments*, Santa Monica, Calif.: RAND Corporation, RR-A958-1, 2021.

[2] Pew Research Center, "Views of Foreign Policy," Pew Research Center, December 17, 2019.

[3] The White House, *U.S. Strategic Framework for the Indo-Pacific*, Washington, D.C., December 2017.

[4] The White House, 2021c, pp. 11, 15.

consistent approach that over time will reduce expenditures and strains on the U.S. military.

Such a comprehensive Middle East security strategy document will focus U.S. activities, explain intentions; and let allies, adversaries, and the American public know what to expect. It will also communicate to the American people what U.S. interests in the Middle East are and how the U.S. government will manage them. Given the recent decades of high military expenditure and wars in the Middle East, as well as a new emphasis on reducing the military footprint, we view a document that describes priorities and approaches to the American public about this region as needed and timely. Voters have indicated that they are confused about U.S. foreign policy objectives, what the United States is trying to achieve in the world, and what the U.S. role is in the Middle East.[5] A public Middle East strategy would better help to remediate this.

Creating a public strategy comes with risks that need to be managed. Risks include the effect on partners (not having adverse reactions to deprioritization of their key interests) or adversaries (who could use certain levels of information to prepare). One way to mitigate these risks is to ensure that the level of information provided does not undermine objectives, with the public version balancing the need for a clear direction without providing too much information to adversaries.

The strategy should be led by the White House through an interagency process, bringing together DoD, the State Department, USAID, the Department of Commerce, the Department of Energy, the U.S. Trade Representative, and others as appropriate.

Develop Substitute Approaches to Manage Risks When Reducing the U.S. Military Footprint in the Middle East

Amid a review of the U.S. global force posture in 2021 with a presidential mandate to "right-size" U.S. military presence in the Middle East, there are

---

[5] John Halpin, Brian Katulis, Peter Juul, Karl Agne, Jim Gerstein, and Nisha Jain, "America Adrift: How the U.S. Foreign Policy Debate Misses What Voters Really Want," Washington, D.C.: Center for American Progress, May 5, 2019.

loud calls for reduction in the U.S. military presence in the Middle East to pivot resources to Asia. This report has made the case that the Middle East is a priority region for U.S. security interests. At the same time, the security context in the Middle East is changing, as outlined in this report, and use of military tools should evolve accordingly. Yet any reduction in the U.S. military footprint should include careful plans for substitute approaches to manage risks, such as alternative military approaches or more sustained investment in diplomatic, economic, and technical assistance tools, and it should be in line with the strategy recommended above. Indeed, there are some security concerns that cannot be addressed by the military at all.

Withdrawal or retrenchment, if not done deliberately with attention to ensuring that risks will be managed through other means, could result in short-sighted policies that neglect American security interests and lead to resurgent risks. As illustrated in Table 1.1, the United States has repeated a pattern of withdrawing without managing risks, followed by new military engagement; this pattern should stop. Those who are calling for restraint or retrenchment have not fully developed the policy implications of what this would mean now in the Middle East, terms under which the United States would re-engage, or implications several steps out.[6]

In particular, there are some key risks that could result from hasty withdrawal or reductions to the U.S. military footprint. These include the following:

- Iran could be incentivized to escalate attacks if it views the United States as less committed to protecting its interests in the region and increase activities through its proxy forces in Iraq, Lebanon, Yemen, Syria, or elsewhere. Iran may also threaten U.S. partners and allies with ballistic missiles and become emboldened to conduct additional strikes on Gulf energy resources.
- The U.S. presence creates confidence in its partners and reins in their military activities; if they view the United States as less present or

---

[6] Miranda Priebe, Bryan Rooney, Nathan Beauchamp-Mustafaga, Jeffrey Martini, Stephanie Pezard, *Implementing Restraint: Changes in U.S. Regional Security Policies to Operationalize a Realist Grand Strategy of Restraint*, Santa Monica, Calif.: RAND Corporation, RR-A739, 2021.

committed, they could strike out defensively against Iran, leading to repercussions that draw the United States in once again.

- Weak capacity in regional governments in combination with a lighter U.S. presence could create space for terrorism to resurge, as has happened after previous U.S. withdrawals from Iraq.
- Dependable allies who have supported the United States in achieving its goals in the past, such as Kurdish groups in Iraq and Syria, may be less willing to take on those roles if they lose trust in the United States as a reliable partner.
- If Middle East governments view the United States as less reliable and committed, they may turn more to China and Russia for weapons sales and other collaborations.
- U.S. weapons sales to the Middle East, which support the U.S. defense industrial base, could decline.
- The United States could lose its ability for rapid reaction it if had a lower presence.
- Reducing the footprint may not achieve as much as hoped in terms of lower costs; indeed, the Gulf states absorb much of the cost for U.S. presence there.

With these considerations in mind, as the United States pulls back militarily, it should do so deliberately, planning for addressing the consequences of such changes and ensure that substitute approaches remain to manage U.S. interests. Course corrections should respond to conditions on the ground, while conditions-free deadlines should be avoided without a dire need to cut costs or move troops elsewhere. There are several ways that this can be done deliberately.

First, DoD should align U.S. force posture in the Middle East with the interagency strategy recommended above, as well as considering ways to provide the same capabilities less expensively. This could include reducing capabilities that are no longer required in the current threat environment, substituting more economically efficient approaches, or increasing security cooperation and partner capacity building. In so doing, the United States should be careful of sending mixed messages to allies, as they will likely follow the U.S. lead in force posture changes. Large-scale abrupt changes could leave Middle East partners vulnerable. While this report does not prescribe the best mix of approaches to cut costs while managing risks, other experts have identified multiple options for doing so.[7] These include

Rotations: The United States could deploy forces in smaller groups in less predictable cycles with shorter rotations and to nontraditional destinations. It could shift to unpredictable short-term rotations of aircraft carrier groups normally in the Indo-Pacific in order to complicate Iran's decisionmaking.

Offloading additional responsibilities to regional partners: The United States could share additional maritime responsibilities, such as those related to energy and trade, with partners to reduce the Gulf naval presence, while keeping a smaller U.S. naval presence there. It could work with partners to maintain the military infrastructure needed to enable rapid U.S. deployment in case of a crisis.

Regional ballistic missile defenses: In view of the progress made through the Abraham Accords, the United States could collaborate with the Gulf states and Israel to develop ballistic missile defenses against Iran. It could also develop more cost effective technology and create responsibilities that are managed in a shared way by these states.

New approaches to intelligence, surveillance, and reconnaissance (ISR): The United States could rely more on satellites, regional governmental assets, and U.S. forces based in Europe. It could further help partner nations develop better ISR capabilities related to terrorism and Iranian activities. For instance, it could develop regional shared ISR capabilities to interdict Iranian arms shipments to proxy forces or have early warning systems against missiles.

---

[7] Steven Simon and Richard Sokolsky, "What to Do With U.S. Forces in the Persian Gulf," *Foreign Policy*, April 16, 2021; John W. Miller, "Biden's Mideast Drawdown Poses Perils," *Defense News*, April 15, 2021; Ari Cicurel, "Biden Should Aim for a Smaller, but Smarter, Military Posture in Middle East," *The Hill*, November 20, 2020; Christine McVann, "Reshaping U.S. Force Posture in the Middle East," Washington, D.C.: The Washington Institute for Near East Policy, March 10, 2021; Robert Burns, "Pentagon Rethinking How to Array Forces to Focus on China," Associated Press, February 17, 2021; Frederic Wehrey, Michele Dunne, Robert Springborg, Emile Hokayem, Becca Wasser, Jodi Vittori, Jonathan D. Caverley, Hassan Maged, Jalel Harchaoui, Andrew S. Weiss, Patricia M. Kim, "How to Rethink America's Middle East Security Strategy," Washington, D.C.: Carnegie Endowment for International Peace, May 18, 2021.

Maintaining some strategic presence: The United States could keep its forces in the Gulf, given that many costs are covered by Gulf partners and that this presence serves as a deterrence to Iran, reassures U.S. partners of its commitment, and enables fast responses when they are needed.

Second, DoD could increase its security cooperation with partners in the Middle East as it reduces its presence. In recent years, planning for DoD security cooperation efforts has been assessed as being ad hoc, with inconsistent incorporation of strategic and partner-level goals into security cooperation planning and insufficient knowledge of which approaches are most effective with particular partners.[8] As the United States lessens its military footprint in the Middle East, it should refocus on the quality of its engagement activity. There are multiple options to do so, including:[9]

Refocused engagements: DoD could refocus the quality of engagement activity with partner militaries, with a lower volume of activities, while making them more meaningful and keeping the critical activities that partners depend upon. It could work with partners to agree on the top ways to work together to meet their priorities and U.S. top priorities, such as exercises, ministerial meetings, presence for security cooperation, and military sales.

Political-military relationships: The United States should make sure that the political-military relationship with partners remains strong, so that leaders know each other and can solve problems quickly. This could be done by maintaining high-level engagement in ministries, operational-level meetings, and senior military dialogue and could also include increased international military education and training, institutional capacity building, leadership training, offering advisers at multiple levels, and coordinating with allies and partners about sharing responsibilities.

Building partner capacity: The United States could place further emphasis on helping regional security institutions improve their management,

---

[8] Jefferson P. Marquis, Michael J. McNerney, S. Rebecca Zimmerman, Merrie Archer, Jeremy Boback, and David Stebbins, *Developing an Assessment, Monitoring, and Evaluation Framework for U.S. Department of Defense Security Cooperation*, Santa Monica, Calif.: RAND Corporation, RR-1611-AME, 2016.

[9] We appreciate discussions with RAND colleague Jennifer Moroney for some of this analysis. See also Simon Sokolsky, 2021; Miller, 2021; Cicurel, 2020; McVann, 2021; Burns, 2021; Wehrey et al., 2021.

personnel, logistics, engineering, and other capabilities, as well as improving the complexity of exercises. There may be particular opportunities for increased collaboration with the Gulf countries in capacity building, as most security cooperation to date with them has focused on foreign military sales. While much of U.S. security cooperation and partner capacity building has been related to countering terrorism, it should now include building partners' capacity to contain Iran and to reduce their vulnerability to Iranian aggression and sponsoring of proxy forces; this is particularly important for Iraq and Lebanon.

Weapons sales: The United States could further target U.S. weapons sales to enable partners to take on more responsibilities in ISR, internal stability, related in particular to dealing with Iranian proxies, anti-terrorism activities, and ballistic missile defenses. It could also review the sales to ensure transparency and that they conform with American values. It could also involve allies and partners in co-development and co-production of capabilities.

Third, the renewed strategy might call for a fresh look at the overall amount of military assistance that the United States gives to different countries. The United States currently gives the largest amount of military assistance to Israel, Egypt, and Jordan as part of previous Middle East peace accords.[10] This substantial assistance may or may not remain as important in the context of the new Middle East strategy. The current emphasis could remain important for reasons such as maintaining views of the United States as a steady and reliable long-term partner, the importance of Israel to countering Iran, the "qualitative military edge" of Israel over neighboring militaries, which the United States has codified into law, the central role of Jordan as a stable partner near the instability in neighboring Syria and Lebanon, the benefits that the United States receives in interoperability with stable allies, and continued partnership with Egypt along with prevention of its turning to Russia.[11] On the other hand, changes might be considered. Given Egypt's

---

[10] Kaye et al., 2021.

[11] On the specific issue of Israel's qualitative military edge, see Jeremy M. Sharp, Jim Zanotti, Kenneth Katzman, Christina L. Arabia, and Clayton Thomas, *Israel's Qualitative Military Edge and Possible U.S. Arms Sales to the United Arab Emirates*, Washington, D.C.: Congressional Research Service, R46580, October 26, 2020.

lack of strong economic reforms, growing autocracy, and sometimes ineffective counterterrorism efforts, the U.S. relationship with that country could evolve—negatively through neglecting points of disagreement or positively if both countries renew efforts to find an accommodation.[12] If it turns out that assistance is not consistent with the U.S. Middle East interagency strategy, then any changes should be made in discussion with partners, in ways that do not leave them vulnerable or skeptical of future U.S. intentions or support.

Maintain an Integrated, Long-Term Strategy with Regard to Iran

Iran remains one of the most important security challenges to the United States. Although Iran policy appears to be among the most volatile as U.S. administrations change, there has actually been significant continuity in overall goals and some methods (such as the use of comprehensive sanctions as leverage). There has, however, been a failure to capture the lessons and gains of previous administrations. Two, in particular, stand out: First, Iran is remarkably resilient to pressure and will be strongly resistant to compromising its goals, and so the ability to walk away from talks and establish containment strategies will be needed as a contingency to reaching a deal. Second, the United States loses by failure to fully coordinate with its allies and partners on the front line facing Iran, and working in greater coordination with them likely means a more durable solution to the challenges from Iran.

While negotiations with Iran are ongoing with rapidly changing circumstances, we suggest several principles for dealing with Iran.

The United States should keep both nuclear nonproliferation and the fuller set of strategic interests, in mind in dealing with Iran. These interests include addressing Iran's ballistic missiles, sponsorship of proxy militias, attacks on U.S. bases and troops, cyberattacks, stoking of sectarian tensions, ongoing toxic and destabilizing competition with Saudi Arabia, and competition for influence with the United States in Iraq. Analysts have advocated

---

[12] Jon B. Alterman, *Making Choices: The Future of the U.S.-Egyptian Relationship*, Washington, D.C.: Center for Strategic and International Studies, August 2016.

for either focusing only on nuclear issues in the near term or for including the full range or Iranian behaviors in negotiations. U.S. officials should use whatever tactics are feasible in the short term, while bearing in mind longer-term objectives of managing these issues.

Second, a containment and de-escalation approach, as opposed to a more aggressive regime-change approach, could manage risks for the United States while checking Iran's most threatening activities and allowing it to overextend itself economically, as its own internal domestic dissatisfaction grows. This approach could include supporting other countries in the region in their ability to maintain security within their borders (particularly Iraq and Lebanon), so that Iran finds less fertile ground in support of militias and fewer openings for interference in their internal affairs.[13] Targeting regime change—even by targeting it *in effect* through requirements that can be satisfied only by such change—is not a solid strategy for several reasons: It is not very likely to succeed; regime changes in the Middle East in recent decades, even when an amoral authoritarian despot is deposed, have been extremely destabilizing with long-term negative repercussions; and such efforts put Iran on an even more aggressive path.

Third, the United States could explore opportunities to "expand the pie," collaborating on areas of mutual interest with Iran and building some trust accordingly. One promising area is collaboration on helping Iran mitigate climate change impacts, such as water shortages and air quality problems in exchange for some change in Iran's behavior.

Fourth, rather than dialing back American force posture in the Middle East for the sake of budgets or pivoting toward Asia, the United States should ensure that its force posture and security cooperation are sufficient to support allies and partners in containing Iran until there is an agreement with Iran that mitigates such risks.

And fifth, a particular longer-term objective should be to calm, if not eventually end, the ongoing rivalry between Iran and Saudi Arabia, as the mutual fueling of proxy groups is one of the most destabilizing factors in ongoing Middle East conflicts. Doing so may involve additional positive and negative incentives for Saudi Arabia or Iran, with an easing of tension being part of the trade space of other issues to be negotiated.

---

[13] Kaye et al., 2021.

Mediate the End of Conflicts and Broker Pragmatic Solutions to Civilian Displacement

The Middle East's many festering conflicts are harming the people of the region, posing risks to U.S. security interests, and spilling over to affect other allies and partners. The United States has had recent successes in supporting the end of conflicts, in particular in leading the coalition to support Iraq in defeating ISIS, facilitating the Abraham Accords, and mediating a reduction in tension between Saudi Arabia and Qatar. Now is the time to turn renewed attention to other festering conflicts in the Middle East that have received less diplomatic attention in recent years, such as those in Libya, Yemen, and Syria.

A next priority for the United States should be leading diplomatic efforts to resolve these conflicts, although some may not be ripe for resolution. Conflict resolution in these cases are faced with multiple constraints, such as the need to negotiate with despots or other violent actors, interference from Iran, and deep disagreements. Yet, ending these conflicts is so vital for regional stability and to U.S. security that finding solutions should be a priority. State Department mediation efforts could draw on the full range of tools and incentives that U.S. agencies have to offer: security cooperation, aid, trade, convening diplomatic, security, and economic discussions and agreements, climate change assistance, alliances, and other resources of power available. Aligned interests may also present opportunities to collaborate with the European Union, Turkey, the Gulf States, and China, and even Russia in the right circumstances, on conflict resolution and stabilization. Even competing states have interests in a stable Middle East and can bring opportunities to the table.

Beyond easing and resolving conflicts, but as important, the United States should lead an effort to find durable solutions for all refugees and IDPs in the Middle East in the next ten years. The region's 20.5 million forcibly displaced people live in abominable conditions without any concrete plans for their futures. While conflicts are ongoing—and even if conflicts are resolved—most will not be able to obtain the solutions that are supposed to be available to them in United Nations policy without a greater U.S. push: returning home, finding a spot in a resettlement country such as the United States or in Europe, or being able to fully participate in their host country societies, with adults having the right to work and children having access to education. The United States should double down on increasing access to these solutions. In addition, new, "out-of-the-box" solutions are needed beyond these typical three options. In particular, the United States should broker arrangements for medium-term work visas for the displaced in countries in the Middle East, Europe, Asia, Latin America, and Africa and should press for countries that typically take few refugees for resettlement, such as those in Asia, Latin America, or Africa, to match U.S. resettlement numbers. To be sure, all of these solutions will depend on incentivizing reluctant states to collaborate, as well as on creative U.S. diplomacy.

Focus U.S. Development Assistance on Addressing Two Main Causes of Arab Spring Protests

The Arab Spring protests, along with the Arab Spring 2.0 a decade later, have led to instability, government overthrows, and civil wars, with results that create security challenges for the United States and its allies and partners. It is in U.S. national security interests to help the Middle East overcome these challenges. In particular, the United States should focus its development assistance on addressing two of the biggest drivers of Arab Spring protests and their aftermath—namely, the lack of economic opportunities for youth and problems of corruption within governments, and with police in particular. While the United States has sporadically provided assistance aimed at improving democracy in Middle East countries, this should not be the priority. To be sure, addressing the lack of opportunity for youth is not easy; nor is addressing corruption, especially not when some governments may have little interest in significant changes in transparency. Yet, U.S. foreign assistance in comparison with military assistance has been slim in general. Addressing these two goals could be a good option for increased levels of overall investment, engagement, and foreign assistance.

In support of job opportunities, the United States could target assistance both for supply and demand for workers. Related to supply, investments could focus on improving the quality of K–12 education and of career and technical education to enable high school graduates to have skills needed by employers; educational exchange between universities would also be benefi-

63

cial. Countries of the Middle East overinvest in university education (with high rates of unemployment among the university educated) and underinvest in career and technical education, which could provide skills needed for more jobs.[14] Education is also a field where the United States could harness capabilities of allies to help; for instance, Germany is particularly adept at offering foreign assistance in career and technical education through the German Agency for International Cooperation. To address the demand side of the labor market, the United States could provide technical assistance to governments to make the economic reforms needed for expansion of private-sector job opportunities, encourage governments of countries with high proportions of less-skilled workers to promote labor-intensive manufacturing strategies, and expand trade agreements. The United States should also initiate additional collaboration among countries within the Middle East, incentivizing richer countries in the region (such as in the Gulf) to invest in the poorer countries and to help with reforms needed to improve the business environment. For example, the United Arab Emirates is one of the few Middle Eastern countries rated high in the ease of doing business; the United States could facilitate the United Arab Emirates providing technical assistance in the types of changes that other countries should undertake. Furthermore, the United States can forge deeper economic integration with the region to facilitate U.S. trade and investment, such as by considering a regional trade agreement or region-wide development funds.

To address corruption, the United States could invest in technical assistance related to rule of law, justice, policing, and transparency and accountability within government functions. Improving policing is a particular area where the United States can encourage allies and partners to help, such as Canada and Italy, which have provided policing training in Iraq. The United States could also provide technical assistance from the State Department Bureau of International Narcotics and Law Enforcement Affairs and from the Department of Commerce on legal and regulatory reform, such as through the Commercial Law Development Program and Anti-Trust Legislation.

---

[14] Louay Constant, Shelly Culbertson, Cathy Stasz, and Georges Vernez, *Improving Technical Vocational Education and Training in the Kurdistan Region—Iraq*, Santa Monica, Calif.: RAND Corporation, RR-277-KRG, 2014; Kumar et al., 2018.

Improve Trust in the United States as a Strong, Effective, Reliable Partner of Choice

In recent years, the positive opinion of the United States globally and in the Middle East has declined, while negative views of the United States as a threat, as a partner that abandons its allies, as weak in foreign policy, and as inconsistent or unreliable have been on the rise. As Dobbins, Tarini, and Wyne note, "Over the past two decades, the United States experienced a dramatic drop-off in international achievement. A generation of Americans have come of age in an era in which foreign policy setbacks have been more frequent than advances."[15]

This is a problem for several reasons. First, it is a reflection of U.S. inconsistency, militarized and transactional engagement, and policies that are not as effective as they might be. Second, meeting security goals in the Middle East depends on the quality of relationships and partnerships with allies and partners, as well as regard for U.S. capability to take leadership to solve vexing problems. Third, it behooves the United States to maintain strong relations with allies and partners in the region in the context of remaining the partner of choice in comparison with Russia and China. Beyond the broad benefits of greater cooperation, there are specific benefits when it comes to U.S. military and security goals. Trust in the United States maintains acceptance of and reliance on U.S. equipment and technology, as opposed to that from Russia and China. The United States is the largest arms supplier to the Middle East, with the region accounting for a third of U.S. arms exports. Arms sales are an important tool for policy influence.[16] Interoperability with regional militaries helps the United States maintain its military advantage; it is better if countries of the region are purchasing U.S. equipment instead of that of other powers.

Being viewed as a strong, trusted, reliable, and measured ally and partner is important for U.S. longer-term security interests in the Middle East. Approaches that meet security interests, maintain American values, and

---

[15] Dobbins, Tarini, and Wyne, 2020.

[16] Dominic Dudley, "U.S. Arms Sales to the Middle East Have Soared in Value This Year," *Forbes*, December 16, 2019; Thomas et al., 2020.

avoid inconsistent "yo-yo" policies[17] may help to smooth U.S. relations, improve partnerships with countries in the region over time, and improve Middle East public opinion about the United States. In this way, the United States can maintain its position as the partner of choice and restore its image in the region as a type of society that is trusted, respected, and admired. Of course, transition of power in a democracy means that different administrations have a mandate to take foreign policy in different directions, but the dramatic swings in policy and military activity in recent decades in the Middle East have not served the United States or the Middle East well.

Maintain an Integrated Program for Countering Violent Extremism

While ISIS has been defeated territorially, violent extremism from Salafist-Jihadists remains a risk to manage for the long term. While some military approaches will be necessary to manage this issue, additional investment in civilian approaches, integrated with military approaches, may be able to address these threats in a more consistent and effective way. We recommend an interagency, coordinated strategy that includes the State Department, USAID, and DoD and targets approaches by country or subregion. While such an interagency strategy was developed in 2016, it was not implemented, and budgets for this purpose at the State Department and USAID were reduced, leaving a mainly militarized approach instead of addressing the wider issues that may contribute to radicalization.[18] Such an integrated program could include the following.

First, a better understanding is needed of effective techniques for deradicalization, apart from military interventions, along the whole chain of violent extremism, from sympathy for extremist causes, to radicalization, to joining a radical group, and to carrying out attacks. Effective deradicalization may involve greater emphasis on addressing issues hypothesized to be involved in radicalization, such as unemployment, low-quality education,

---

[17] Ilan Goldenberg, "America's Yo-Yo Diet in the Middle East," *Politico Magazine*, December 19, 2018.

[18] Eric Rosand, "International Efforts to Counter Violent Extremism Under President Trump: A Case Study in Dysfunction and Incoherence," Brookings, September 9, 2020.

inspiration through social media, the desire to protect one's own community, or other causes. It also may involve developing better tools to counteract online recruitment and inspiration.

Second, as United States military continues its targeted efforts against extremist groups in coordination with regional governments, it could also place more emphasis on supporting regional government efforts in countering violent extremism, including through capacity building of law enforcement agencies, civil society organizations, and special operations and other specialized forces.

Third, the United States should take the lead on coordinating a multilateral solution for imprisoned ISIS fighters and families with perceived ISIS affiliations in camps in Syria and Iraq, such as Al-Hol. This would involve continuing to fund security for the camps and collaborating with the government of Iraq, the Kurdistan Regional Government in Iraq, the Autonomous Administration of North and East Syria, and other concerned governments, such as governments of citizens in the camps, including European governments, Russia, and Turkey. Justice procedures to adjudicate who has committed crimes are needed, as are dealing with the thousands of children being raised in such a radicalized environment, moving those who have committed no crimes back into civilian life, and ensuring secure long-term solutions for violent terrorists.

Facilitate Regional Interactions, Mutual Assistance, and Security Dialogues

Sustaining, repairing, and drawing upon the vast U.S. network of allies and partners will be a priority for managing American security interests in the Middle East. There are multiple issues that would benefit from regional security discussions, or where allies and partners could assist with their comparative advantages. The Middle East is the only region without a functioning forum for security dialogue and cooperation on other issues of importance.[19] The Abraham Accords offers opportunities to bring Israel into such an arrangement.

---

[19] Perry Cammack and Michele Dunne. "Fueling Middle East Conflicts—or Dousing the Flames," Washington, D.C.: Carnegie Endowment for International Peace, 2018.

Both the Obama and Trump administrations supported the proposed MESA, which aims to integrate military, energy, political, and economic security and present additional new opportunities for regional discussions and problem-solving.[20] However, the initiative never got off the ground because of disagreements about its scope, with the United States pressing to include a wide range of interests and several Arab nations wanting it to include only security.[21] The Biden administration should revive discussions and also aim to bring in Israel and Turkey. Doing so could be important in jump-starting a regional dialogue on peace and security, resolving ongoing civil wars, developing common regional approaches to ISR related to intercepting Iranian arms shipments to its proxies, developing common regional approaches to ballistic missile defenses against Iran and its proxies, developing durable solutions for refugees and the internally displaced (such as returns or expanded work visas), de-escalating rivalries between Iran and Saudi Arabia, finding regional solutions to improve economies and increase quality job opportunities for youth, and facilitating wealthier Middle East countries in helping lower-income countries with economic reforms. The United States could also encourage other partners and allies to take leading roles on issues of interest. For instance, the United States could encourage the United Arab Emirates to provide technical assistance on business climate reforms and offer a clearinghouse for lessons learned in deregulation and labor market innovations.

Invest in Encouraging the Linchpin Countries of Iraq and Tunisia on the Path to Success

Two countries in the Middle East merit a special push for U.S. technical assistance: Iraq and Tunisia. It is important for the future stability of the Middle East and U.S. national security interests for these two countries to succeed in improving governance and economic opportunities for their citizens. In a region of conflicts and quagmires, supporting a successful Iraq and Tunisia would provide an important source of hope and stability, even

---

[20] Yasmine Farouk, "The Middle East Strategic Alliance Has a Long Way To Go," Washington, D.C.: Carnegie Endowment for International Peace, February 8, 2019.

[21] Kirsten Fontenrose, "How Joe Biden Hopes to Shift U.S. Policy in the Middle East," *The National Interest*, January 31, 2021.

as both present significant challenges to doing so because of their complicated political dynamics and economies that are weighed down by corruption and cronyism. This would mean facilitating their success on the basis of their needs—security, economic reforms, technical assistance, and judicial and justice assistance.

Iraq is a U.S. strategic partner and is recovering from war with ISIS and from the U.S.-led 2003 Iraq War. Iraqis take great pride that they provided the world a global good through their efforts to defeat ISIS, with U.S. and coalition support. There are also signs that sectarianism is on the wane in light of this national triumph. It is important for the Middle East to have an example of a country that has recovered from war, improved stability, and prospered. Iraq is a functioning democracy (albeit with significant troubles) and has embarked on a renewed effort to reform its economy as outlined in its *White Paper for Economic Reform*.[22] Iraq faces a steep climb in rebuilding after war and addressing issues such as rampant corruption that stymie its economy and hinder foreign investment. In addition, Iranian regional power depends in part on its influence in a weak Iraq. Although Iraq benefits from engaging with Iran, it also does not want to be dominated or unduly influenced by it. It is in American interests to serve as a counterweight to Iran in support of Iraq.

Tunisia is the only country, after overthrowing its government during the Arab Spring, to embark on the kinds of initiatives that address the causes of the protests. Given frustration with Tunisia's former authoritarian regime, it is perhaps no coincidence that Tunisia is both where Arab Spring protests started and the country that produced the most foreign fighters per capita for ISIS (although this second issue can also be attributed to the postrevolutionary government's inability to control its borders).[23] After its revolution in 2011, Tunisia's secular and Islamist parties formed a unity government, developed a new constitution based on both democratic and Islamist values, and made difficult progress in improving governance and accountability. However, Tunisia's economy remains stagnant and is not providing

---

[22] Government of Iraq, *White Paper for Economic Reform (Final Report of the Crisis Cell for Financial and Fiscal Reform)*, Baghdad, October 2020; Government of Iraq, *White Paper for Economic Reform, Volume II—Reform Implementation Plan, Part One: Governance, Part Two: Projects*, Baghdad, January 2021.

[23] Ian Bremmer, "The Top Five Countries Where ISIS Gets Its Foreign Recruits," *Time*, April 14, 2017.

adequate jobs for its youth. The Middle East needs an example of a country that has addressed Arab Spring demands successfully and put its youth on a track to better opportunities.

Looking Ahead: A New U.S. Approach to a New Middle East

U.S. involvement in the Middle East stretches back hundreds of years, to even before the U.S. Constitution was approved and George Washington became the first president.[24] While the United States has had long-term interests in safeguarding the free flow of oil to global markets, reducing terrorism risks, and countering Iran, regional changes suggest several new interests. These changes call for new approaches that better safeguard U.S. security, build better partnerships, and gain economic benefits for Americans.

In this report, we have outlined a renewed U.S. strategic approach, placing greater emphasis on diplomatic, economic, and technical assistance tools than on military tools, while at the same time deliberately recalibrating military tools to ensure both that threats are addressed and that resources can be saved to shift some focus to Asia. This new approach can be judged to be effective or at least contributing to these goals in the coming years if the Middle East sees reduced internal unrest and conflict and improved economic and social indicators and if the United States has reduced casualties and expenditures in managing these risks.

The populations of the Middle East have demonstrated their ability to sacrifice for development and for a better, more prosperous, more peaceful life. Helping deliver these goals should be a U.S. interest. The United States can do so by actively working to end conflicts and by helping foster greater economic exchange and more effective government. And doing so will also lower the risk that the United States will be called up once again to engage in military operations in the region, with their attendant high costs. A reshaped U.S. strategy that both maintains the Middle East as a priority and rebalances its military and civilian tools can help steer the region from one where costs to the United States prevail to one where benefits to the American people emerge.

---

[24] Office of the Historian, undated b; Oren, 2011.

References

Al-Kinani, Mohammed, "Saudi Arabia Must Be Involved in Fresh Talks on Iran Deal, Says Macron," *Arab News*, January 29, 2021. As of February 20, 2021:
https://www.arabnews.com/node/1800536/middle-east

Alterman, Jon B., *Making Choices: The Future of the U.S.-Egyptian Relationship*, Washington, D.C.: Center for Strategic and International Studies, August 2016. As of May 19, 2021:
https://www.csis.org/analysis/making-choices-future-us-egyptian-relationship

———, *The Other Side of the World: China, the United States, and the Struggle for Middle East Security*, Washington, D.C.: Center for Strategic and International Studies, March 2017. As of March 15, 2021:
https://csis-website-prod.s3.amazonaws.com/s3fs-public/publication/170303
_Alterman_OtherSideOfWorld_Web.pdf

———, "Chinese and Russian Influence in the Middle East," statement before the House Foreign Affairs Subcommittee on the Middle East, North Africa, and International Terrorism, Washington, D.C.: Center for Strategic and International Studies, May 9, 2019. As of March 15, 2021:
https://csis-website-prod.s3.amazonaws.com/s3fs-public/congressional
_testimony/190509_Alterman-Testimony.pdf

———, "Pivoting to Asia Doesn't Get You Out of the Middle East," Washington, D.C.: Center for Strategic and International Studies, October 19, 2020. As of February 16, 2021:
https://www.csis.org/analysis/pivoting-asia-doesnt-get-you-out-middle-east

Amer, Adnan Abu, "Hamas Opens Up on Arms, Missile Supplies from Iran," *Al-Monitor*, September 24, 2020. As of February 21, 2021:
https://www.al-monitor.com/pulse/originals/2020/09/hamas-reveal-military
-secret-weapons-smuggling.html

American Security Project, "U.S. Bases in the Middle East," interactive map, February 9, 2021. As of February 18, 2021:
https://www.americansecurityproject.org/national-security-strategy/u-s
-bases-in-the-middle-east/

Arab Center Washington, D.C., "The 2019–2020 Arab Opinion Index: Main Results in Brief," webpage, November 16, 2020. As of March 12, 2021:
http://arabcenterdc.org/survey/the-2019-2020-arab-opinion-index-main
-results-in-brief/

Arms Control Association, "Nuclear Weapons: Who Has What at a Glance," Fact Sheets and Briefs, August 2020. As of February 20, 2021:
https://www.armscontrol.org/factsheets/Nuclearweaponswhohaswhat

ASDA'A BCW, *Arab Youth Survey: A Decade of Hopes and Fears*, 2018.

Azeng, Therese F., and Thierry U. Yogo, *Youth Unemployment and Political Instability in Selected Developing Countries*, Belvédère, Tunisia: African Development Bank, Group Working Paper Series No. 171, May 2013.

Bacevich, Andrew J., *America's War for the Greater Middle East: A Military History*, New York: Random House, 2016.

Baffa, Richard C., Nathan Vest, Wing Yi Chan, and Abby Fanlo, *Defining and Understanding the Next Generation of Salafi-Jihadis*, Santa Monica, Calif.: RAND Corporation, PE-341-ODNI, 2019. As of March 12, 2021: https://www.rand.org/pubs/perspectives/PE341.html

Bagchi, Aniruddha, and Jomon Paul, "Youth Unemployment and Terrorism in the MENAP (Middle East, North Africa, Afghanistan, and Pakistan) Region," *Socio-Economic Planning Sciences*, Vol. 64, December 2018, pp. 9–20.

Barrett, Richard, *Beyond the Caliphate: Foreign Fighters and the Threat of Returnees*, New York: Soufan Group, October 2017.

Beckwith, Ryan Teague, "Read Donald Trump's 'America First' Foreign Policy Speech," *Time*, April 27, 2016. As of March 15, 2021: https://time.com/4309786/read-donald-trumps-america-first-foreign-policy -speech/

Benaim, Daniel, and Jake Sullivan, "America's Opportunity in the Middle East: Diplomacy Could Succeed Where Military Force Has Failed," *Foreign Affairs*, May 22, 2020. As of May 11, 2021: https://www.foreignaffairs.com/articles/middle-east/2020-05-22/americas -opportunity-middle-east

Bertuca, Tony, "Austin Pledges to Include Climate Change Review in Upcoming National Defense Strategy," *Inside Defense*, January 27, 2021. As of March 15, 2021: https://insidedefense.com/daily-news/austin-pledges-include-climate-change -review-upcoming-national-defense-strategy

Biden for President, "The Power of America's Example: The Biden Plan for Leading the Democratic World to Meet the Challenges of the 21st Century," webpage, undated. As of March 12, 2021: https://joebiden.com/americanleadership/

Blackwill, Robert D., *Trump's Foreign Policies Are Better Than They Seem*, Council Special Report No. 84, Council on Foreign Relations, April 2019. As of May 18, 2021: https://www.cfr.org/report/trumps-foreign-policies-are-better-they-seem

Blanchard, Christopher M., *Libya: Conflict, Transition, and U.S. Policy*, Washington, D.C.: Congressional Research Service, RL33142, June 26, 2020.

Bock, Alan, "Reagan's Wisdom on the Middle East: Leave," *Orange County Register*, July 21, 2006. As of March 12, 2021:
https://www.ocregister.com/2006/07/21/reagans-wisdom-on-the-middle-east-leave/

Bowlus, John V., "Eastern Mediterranean Gas: Testing the Field," in *Deep Sea Rivals: Europe, Turkey, and New Eastern Mediterranean Conflict Lines*, London: European Council on Foreign Relations, May 2020. As of February 9, 2021:
https://ecfr.eu/special/eastern_med

Bremmer, Ian, "The Top Five Countries Where ISIS Gets Its Foreign Recruits," *Time*, April 14, 2017. As of March 15, 2021:
https://time.com/4739488/isis-iraq-syria-tunisia-saudi-arabia-russia/

British Petroleum, *Statistical Review of World Energy 2020*, 69th Edition, London, June 2020.

Burns, Robert, "Pentagon Rethinking How to Array Forces to Focus on China," Associated Press, February 17, 2021. As of May 14, 2021:
https://apnews.com/article/joe-biden-lloyd-austin-china-russia-united-states-a527916527940705a0aa9fb7d1f36eaf

Bush, George H. W., "Address to the Nation on the Invasion of Iraq," speech, Washington, D.C.: The White House, January 16, 1991. As of February 25, 2021:
https://millercenter.org/the-presidency/presidential-speeches/january-16-1991-address-nation-invasion-iraq

Calabrese, John, "Intersections: China and the U.S. in the Middle East," Washington, D.C.: Middle East Institute, June 18, 2019. As of March 15, 2021:
https://www.mei.edu/publications/intersections-china-and-us-middle-east

Cammack, Perry, and Michele Dunne, "Fueling Middle East Conflicts—or Dousing the Flames," Washington, D.C.: Carnegie Endowment for International Peace, 2018. As of March 16, 2021:
https://carnegieendowment.org/2018/10/23/fueling-middle-east-conflicts-or-dousing-flames-pub-77548

Carpenter, Scott, "New Pipeline Deal Gives Europe Access to Eastern Mediterranean Gas Reserves, Angering Turkey," *Forbes*, January 2, 2020. As of February 16, 2021:
https://www.forbes.com/sites/scottcarpenter/2020/01/02/new-gas-pipeline-deal-gives-europe-access-to-eastern-mediterranean-reserves-angering-turkey/?sh=5f90bdb01c69

Carter, Jimmy, *The State of the Union Address Delivered Before a Joint Session of the Congress*, Washington, D.C.: The White House, January 23, 1980.

CBS News, "Text of Bush Speech," webpage, May 1, 2003. As of February 25, 2021:
https://www.cbsnews.com/news/text-of-bush-speech-01-05-2003/

Chulov, Martin, "ISIS: The Inside Story," *The Guardian*, December 11, 2014.

Cicurel, Ari, "Biden Should Aim for a Smaller, but Smarter, Military Posture in Middle East," *The Hill*, November 20, 2020. As of May 14, 2021: https://thehill.com/opinion/international/526275-biden-should-aim-for-a -smaller-but-smarter-military-posture-in-middle?rl=1

Clarke, Colin P., William Courtney, Bradley Martin, and Bruce McClintock, "Russia Is Eyeing the Mediterranean. The U.S. and NATO Must Be Prepared," *The RAND Blog*, June 30, 2020. As of March 15, 2021: https://www.rand.org/blog/2020/06/russia-is-eyeing-the-mediterranean-the -us-and-nato.html

"Climate Change Is Making the Arab World More Miserable," *The Economist*, June 2, 2018. As of March 15, 2021: https://www.economist.com/middle-east-and-africa/2018/05/31/climate-change -is-making-the-arab-world-more-miserable

Clinton, Bill, "Remarks at the Signing of the Israeli-Palestinian Agreement," video, Washington, D.C.: The White House, September 13, 1993. As of February 25, 2021: https://millercenter.org/the-presidency/presidential-speeches/september-13 -1993-remarks-signing-israeli-palestinian

Cloud, David S., "Inside U.S. Troops' Stronghold in Syria, a Question of How Long Biden Will Keep Them There," *Los Angeles Times*, March 12, 2021. As of March 15, 2021: https://www.latimes.com/politics/story/2021-03-12/us-troops-syria-civil-war -biden

Collins, Shannon, "Desert Storm: A Look Back," *DoD News*, January 11, 2019. As of March 15, 2021: https://www.defense.gov/Explore/Features/story/Article/1728715/desert-storm -a-look-back/

Committee on Nuclear Proliferation, *A Report to the President by the Committee on Nuclear Proliferation*, Washington, D.C., January 21, 1965. As of February 20, 2021: https://history.state.gov/historicaldocuments/frus1964-68v11/d64

Congressional Budget Office, "Federal Budget in 2016: An Infographic," Washington, D.C., 2017.

———, "Federal Budget in 2017: An Infographic," Washington, D.C., 2018.

———, "Federal Budget in 2018: An Infographic," Washington, D.C., 2019.

———, "Federal Budget in 2019: An Infographic," Washington, D.C., 2020.

Connable, Ben, James Dobbins, Howard J. Shatz, Raphael S. Cohen, and Becca Wasser, *Weighing U.S. Troop Withdrawal from Iraq: Strategic Risks and Recommendations*, Santa Monica, Calif.: RAND Corporation, PE-362-OSD, 2020. As of March 1, 2021:
https://www.rand.org/pubs/perspectives/PE362.html

Connor, Phillip, "Most Displaced Syrians Are in the Middle East, and About a Million Are in Europe," *FactTank*, Pew Research Center, January 29, 2018. As of March 12, 2021:
https://www.pewresearch.org/fact-tank/2018/01/29/where-displaced-syrians
-have-resettled/

Constant, Louay, Shelly Culbertson, Cathy Stasz, and Georges Vernez, *Improving Technical Vocational Education and Training in the Kurdistan Region—Iraq*, Santa Monica, Calif.: RAND Corporation, RR-277-KRG, 2014. As of March 15, 2021:
https://www.rand.org/pubs/research_reports/RR277.html

Cornish, Chloe, Asser Khattab, and Henry Foy, "Moscow Collects Its Spoils of War in Assad's Syria," *Financial Times*, September 1, 2019. As of March 16, 2021:
https://www.ft.com/content/30ddfdd0-b83e-11e9-96bd-8e884d3ea203

Crowley, Michael, "Violence in Israel Challenges Biden's 'Stand Back' Approach," *New York Times*, May 11, 2021. As of May 11, 2021:
https://www.nytimes.com/2021/05/11/us/politics/biden-israel-palestinians.html

Culbertson, Shelly, *The Fires of Spring: A Post–Arab Spring Journey Through the Turbulent New Middle East*, New York: St. Martin's Press, 2016.

Culbertson, Shelly, and Louay Constant, *Education of Syrian Refugee Children: Managing the Crisis in Turkey, Lebanon, and Jordan*, Santa Monica, Calif.: RAND Corporation, RR-859-CMEPP, 2015. As of February 25, 2021:
https://www.rand.org/pubs/research_reports/RR859.html

Defense Casualty Analysis System, "U.S. Military Casualties–OCO Casualty Summary by Casualty Type," table, Washington, D.C., March 2, 2021. As of March 2, 2021:
https://dcas.dmdc.osd.mil/dcas/pages/report_sum_reason.xhtml

Delman, Edward, "Obama Promised to End America's Wars—Has He?" *The Atlantic*, March 30, 2016. As of February 25, 2021:
https://www.theatlantic.com/international/archive/2016/03/obama-doctrine
-wars-numbers/474531/

Dobbins, James, Gabrielle Tarini, and Ali Wyne, *The Lost Generation in American Foreign Policy*, Santa Monica, Calif.: RAND Corporation, PE-A232-1, 2020. As of March 15, 2021:
https://www.rand.org/pubs/perspectives/PEA232-1.html

DoD—*See* U.S. Department of Defense.

Doran, Michael, "Obama's Secret Iran Strategy," *Mosaic Magazine*, February 2, 2015. As of February 19, 2021:
https://mosaicmagazine.com/essay/politics-current-affairs/2015/02/obamas-secret-iran-strategy/

Dudley, Dominic, "U.S. Arms Sales to the Middle East Have Soared in Value This Year," *Forbes*, December 16, 2019. As of March 15, 2021:
https://www.forbes.com/sites/dominicdudley/2019/12/16/arms-sales-middle-east-soar/?sh=1f08c75efea8

Edson, José, Ilana Wainer, and Bruno Ferrero, *Final Technical: Regional Desalination and Climate Change*, Abu Dhabi: Abu Dhabi Global Environmental Data Initiative, 2016.

Egel, Daniel, and Trevor Johnston, "Yemen's Chaos Creates a New Opportunity for the Biden-Harris Team," *The National Interest*, November 22, 2020. As of February 21, 2021:
https://nationalinterest.org/feature/yemen%E2%80%99s-chaos-creates-new-opportunity-biden-harris-team-172955

EIA—*See* U.S. Energy Information Administration.

Ellman, Michael, "Iran's Ballistic Missile Program," The Iran Primer, Washington, D.C.: U.S. Institute of Peace, January 13, 2021. As of February 21, 2021:
https://iranprimer.usip.org/resource/irans-ballistic-missile-program

Embassy of the United Arab Emirates, "UAE Supports U.S. President's Decision to Withdraw from Iranian Nuclear Agreement," Washington, D.C., undated. As of February 20, 2021:
https://www.uae-embassy.org/news-media/uae-support-us-president%E2%80%99s-decision-withdraw-iranian-nuclear-agreement

Farmer, Carrie M., Heather Krull, Thomas W. Concannon, Molly M. Simmons, Francesca Pillemer, Teague Ruder, Andrew M. Parker, Maulik P. Purohit, Liisa Hiatt, Benjamin Saul Batorsky, and Kimberly A. Hepner, *Understanding Treatment of Mild Traumatic Brain Injury in the Military Health System*, Santa Monica, Calif.: RAND Corporation, RR-844-OSD, 2016. As of February 25, 2021:
https://www.rand.org/pubs/research_reports/RR844.html

Farouk, Yasmine, "The Middle East Strategic Alliance Has a Long Way to Go," Washington, D.C.: Carnegie Endowment for International Peace, February 8, 2019. As of March 15, 2021:
https://carnegieendowment.org/2019/02/08/middle-east-strategic-alliance-has-long-way-to-go-pub-78317

Fetterolf, Janell, and Jacob Poushter, *Key Middle East Publics See Russia, Turkey and U.S. All Playing Larger Roles in Region*, Washington, D.C.: Pew Research Center, December 11, 2017. As of March 15, 2021:
https://www.pewresearch.org/global/2017/12/11/key-middle-east-publics-see-russia-turkey-and-u-s-all-playing-larger-roles-in-region/

Fontenrose, Kirsten, "How Joe Biden Hopes to Shift U.S. Policy in the Middle East," *The National Interest,* January 31, 2021.

Galbraith, Peter W., "Refugees from War in Iraq: What Happened in 1991 and What May Happen in 2003," Migration Policy Institute, No. 2, February, 2003. As of April 6, 2021:
https://www.migrationpolicy.org/pubs/MPIPolicyBriefIraq.pdf

Gallup, "U.S. Position in the World," Gallup, 2021. As of May 17, 2021:
https://news.gallup.com/poll/116350/position-world.aspx

Gambrell, John, "Here Are the Members of the Saudi-Led Coalition in Yemen and What They're Contributing," *Business Insider,* March 30, 2015. As of February 21, 2021:
https://www.businessinsider.com/members-of-saudi-led-coalition-in-yemen-their-contributions-2015-3

Garamone, Jim, "U.S. Completes Troop-Level Drawdown in Afghanistan, Iraq," *DoD News,* January 15, 2021. As of March 15, 2021:
https://www.defense.gov/Explore/News/Article/Article/2473884/us-completes-troop-level-drawdown-in-afghanistan-iraq/

Garver, John W., *China and Iran: An Emerging Partnership Post-Sanctions,* Washington, D.C.: Middle East Institute, MEI Policy Focus 2016-3, February 2016. As of March 15, 2021:
https://www.jstor.org/stable/resrep17581?seq=1#metadata_info_tab_contents

Gates, Robert M., "The Overmilitarization of American Foreign Policy," *Foreign Affairs,* July/August 2020. As of March 12, 2021:
https://www.foreignaffairs.com/articles/united-states/2020-06-02/robert-gates-overmilitarization-american-foreign-policy

Ghantous, Ghaida, Stephen Kalin, and Sarah Dadouch, "Saudi Arabia Says Backs U.S. Decision to Withdraw from Iran Nuclear Deal," Reuters, May 8, 2018. As of February 20, 2021:
https://www.reuters.com/article/us-iran-nuclear-gulf/saudi-arabia-says-backs-u-s-decision-to-withdraw-from-iran-nuclear-deal-idUSKBN1I92SH

Ghattas, Kim, *Black Wave: Saudi Arabia, Iran, and the Forty-Year Rivalry That Unraveled Culture, Religion, and Collective Memory in the Middle East,* New York: Henry Holt and Company, 2020.

Glenn, Cameron, Mattisan Rowan, John Caves, and Garrett Nada, "Timeline: The Rise, Spread, and Fall of the Islamic State," Washington, D.C.: The Wilson Center, October 28, 2019.

Goldenberg, Ilan, "America's Yo-Yo Diet in the Middle East," *Politico Magazine,* December 19, 2018. As of March 15, 2021:
https://www.politico.com/magazine/story/2018/12/19/americas-yo-yo-diet-in-the-middle-east-223320/

Government of Iraq, *White Paper for Economic Reform (Final Report of the Crisis Cell for Financial and Fiscal Reform)*, Baghdad, October 2020. As of March 15, 2021:
https://gds.gov.iq/iraqs-white-paper-for-economic-reforms-vision-and-key
-objectives/

————, *White Paper for Economic Reform–Volume II–Reform Implementation Plan, Part One: Governance, Part Two: Projects*, Baghdad, January 2021. As of March 15, 2021:
https://gds.gov.iq/iraqi-government-to-begin-implementation-phase-of-the
-white-paper-for-economic-reform/

Halpin, John, Brian Katulis, Peter Juul, Karl Agne, Jim Gerstein, and Nisha Jain, "America Adrift: How the U.S. Foreign Policy Debate Misses What Voters Really Want," Washington, D.C.: Center for American Progress, May 5, 2019. As of May 17, 2021:
https://www.americanprogress.org/issues/security/reports/2019/05/05/469218/
america-adrift/

Hauslohner, Abigail, "Biden Seeks to Restore 'Badly Damaged' Refugee Resettlement Program," *Washington Post*, February 5, 2021.

Holtom, Paul, Mark Bromley, Pieter D. Wezeman, and Siemon T. Wezeman, "Trends in International Arms Transfers, 2012," SIPRI Fact Sheet, Stockholm: Stockholm International Peace Research Institute, March 2013. As of March 15, 2021:
https://www.sipri.org/sites/default/files/files/FS/SIPRIFS1303.pdf

Howard, Jimmy H., *The United States and Saudi Arabia: A Special Relationship; Its Birth, Evolution and Reapportionment*, thesis, Monterey, Calif.: Naval Postgraduate School, June 1981.

Human Rights Watch, "Yemen: Events of 2020," webpage, undated. As of February 19, 2021:
https://www.hrw.org/world-report/2021/country-chapters/yemen

Humud, Carla E., and Christopher M. Blanchard, *Armed Conflict in Syria: Overview and U.S. Response*, Washington, D.C.: Congressional Research Service, RL33487, July 27, 2020.

Ianchovichina, Elena, *Eruptions of Popular Anger: The Economics of the Arab Spring and Its Aftermath*, Washington, D.C.: International Bank for Reconstruction and Development, The World Bank, 2018. As of March 15, 2021:
http://documents1.worldbank.org/curated/en/251971512654536291/pdf/121942
-REVISED-Eruptions-of-Popular-Anger-preliminary-rev.pdf

Indyk, Martin, "The Middle East Isn't Worth It Anymore," *Wall Street Journal*, January 17, 2020. As of February 25, 2021:
https://www.wsj.com/articles/the-middle-east-isnt-worth-it-anymore
-11579277317

Inspector General, *Operation Inherent Resolve: Lead Inspector General Report to the United States Congress*, Washington, D.C., April 1, 2020–June 30, 2020a.

——, *Operation Inherent Resolve: Lead Inspector General Report to the United States Congress*, Washington, D.C., July 1, 2020–September 30, 2020b.

Institute of Medicine (U.S.) Committee on the Initial Assessment of Readjustment Needs of Military Personnel, Veterans, and Their Families, "Operation Enduring Freedom and Operation Iraqi Freedom: Demographics and Impact," in *Returning Home from Iraq and Afghanistan: Preliminary Assessment of Readjustment Needs of Veterans, Service Members, and Their Families*, Washington, D.C.: National Academies Press, 2010.

International Crisis Group, "Exiles in Their Own Country: Dealing with Displacement in Post-ISIS Iraq," Briefing No. 79, October 19, 2020. As of February 25, 2021:
https://www.crisisgroup.org/middle-east-north-africa/gulf-and-arabian
-peninsula/iraq/b79-exiles-their-own-country-dealing-displacement-post
-isis-iraq

International Institute for Strategic Studies, *The Military Balance 2021*, London, February 2021.

Jenkins, Brian Michael, "Options for Dealing with Islamic State Foreign Fighters Currently Detained in Syria," *CTC Sentinel*, Vol. 12, No. 5, May/June 2019.

Kabbani, Nader, *Youth Employment in the Middle East and North Africa: Revisiting and Reframing the Challenge*, Washington, D.C.: The Brookings Institution, February 26, 2019.

Karlin, Mara, and Tamara Cofman Wittes, "America's Middle East Purgatory: The Case for Doing Less," *Foreign Affairs*, January/February 2019. As of March 12, 2021:
https://www.foreignaffairs.com/articles/middle-east/2018-12-11/americas
-middle-east-purgatory

Katz, Mark N., "Same Ends but Different Means: Change, Continuity and Moscow's Middle East Policy," in Karim Mezran and Arturo Varvelli, eds., *The MENA Region: A Great Power Competition*, Milan: ISPI and Atlantic Council, 2019, pp. 39–51. As of March 15, 2021:
https://www.ispionline.it/sites/default/files/pubblicazioni/ispi_report_mena
_region_2019.pdf

Kaye, Dalia Dassa, Linda Robinson, Jeffrey Martini, Nathan Vest, and Ashley L. Rhoades, *Reimagining U.S. Strategy in the Middle East: Sustainable Partnerships, Strategic Investments*, Santa Monica, Calif.: RAND Corporation, RR-A958-1, 2021. As of March 15, 2021:
https://www.rand.org/pubs/research_reports/RRA958-1.html

Kelley, Colin P., Shahrzad Mohtadi, Mark A. Cane, Richard Seager, and Yochanan Kushnir, "Climate Change in the Fertile Crescent and Implications of the Recent Syrian Drought," *Proceedings of the National Academy of Sciences*, Vol. 112, 2015, pp. 3241–3246. As of March 15, 2021:
https://www.pnas.org/content/112/11/3241

Kerr, Paul K., *Iran's Nuclear Program: Tehran's Compliance with International Obligations*, Washington, D.C.: Congressional Research Service, R40094, November 20, 2020.

Kerr, Paul K., and Kenneth Katzman, *Iran Nuclear Agreement and U.S. Exit*, Washington, D.C.: Congressional Research Service, R43333, July 20, 2018.

Kershner, Isabel, "Iran Deal Denounced by Netanyahu as 'Historic Mistake,'" *New York Times*, July 14, 2015. As of February 20, 2021:
https://www.nytimes.com/2015/07/15/world/middleeast/iran-nuclear-deal
-israel.html

Khlebnikov, Alexey, "Russia Looks to the Middle East to Boost Arms Exports," Washington, D.C.: Middle East Institute, April 8, 2019. As of March 15, 2021:
https://www.mei.edu/publications/russia-looks-middle-east-boost-arms
-exports

Kingdom of Saudi Arabia, *Saudi Vision 2030*, Riyadh, 2016; As of March 10, 2021:
https://www.vision2030.gov.sa/en

Kissinger, Henry, *World Order*, London: Penguin, 2015.

Koplow, Michael J., "The Challenge of Solidifying the Abraham Accords," New York: Israel Policy Forum, January 7, 2021. As of May 18, 2021:
https://israelpolicyforum.org/2021/01/07/the-challenge-of-solidifying-the
-abraham-accords/

Korte, Gregory, "Sixteen Times Obama Said There Would Be No Boots on the Ground in Syria," *USA Today*, October 31, 2015.

Kortunov, Andrey, "The Astana Model: Methods and Ambitions of Russian Political Action," in Karim Mezran and Arturo Varvelli, eds., *The MENA Region: A Great Power Competition*, Milan: ISPI and Atlantic Council, 2019, pp. 53–63. As of March 15, 2021:
https://www.ispionline.it/sites/default/files/pubblicazioni/ispi_report_mena
_region_2019.pdf

Koutantou, Angeliki, "Greece, Israel, Cyprus Sign EastMed Gas Pipeline Deal," Reuters, January 2, 2020. As of February 16, 2021:
https://www.reuters.com/article/us-greece-cyprus-israel-pipeline/greece
-israel-cyprus-sign-eastmed-gas-pipeline-deal-idUSKBN1Z10R5

Krafft, Caroline, and Ragui Assaad, "Employment's Role in Enabling and Constraining Marriage in the Middle East and North Africa," *Demography*, Vol. 57, No. 6, 2020, pp. 2297–2325.

Krieger, Tim, and Daniel Meierrieks, "What Causes Terrorism?" *Public Choice*, Vol. 147, No. 1/2, April 2011.

Kumar, Krishna B., Shelly Culbertson, Louay Constant, Shanthi Nataraj, Fatih Unlu, Kathryn E. Bouskill, Joy S. Moini, Katherine Costello, Gursel Rafig oglu Aliyev, and Fadia Afashe, *Opportunities for All: Mutually Beneficial Opportunities for Syrians and Host Countries in Middle Eastern Labor Markets*, Santa Monica, Calif.: RAND Corporation, RR-2653-QFFD, 2018. As of February 25, 2021:
https://www.rand.org/pubs/research_reports/RR2653.html

Lelieveld, Johannes, and Panos Hadjinicolaou, "Climate-Exodus Expected in the Middle East and North Africa," Max-Planck-Gesellschaft, May 2, 2016. As of March 15, 2021:
https://www.mpg.de/10481936/climate-change-middle-east-north-africa

Lelieveld, Jos, Yiannis Proestos, Panos Hadjinicolaou, Meryem Tanarhte, Evangelos Tyrlis, and Georgios Zittis, "Strongly Increasing Heat Extremes in the Middle East and North Africa (MENA) in the 21st Century," *Climatic Change*, Vol. 137, 2016, pp. 245–260.

Levs, Josh, "Iran Leader's Call to 'Annihilate' Israel Sparks Fury as Nuclear Deadline Looms," CNN, November 10, 2014. As of February 20, 2021:
https://www.cnn.com/2014/11/10/world/meast/iran-annihilate-israel

Lister, Charles, "After Five Years of Russian Intervention in Syria," *Asharq Al-Awsat*, August 15, 2020. As of March 15, 2021:
https://english.aawsat.com/home/article/2449526/charles-lister/after-5-years-russian-intervention-syria

Little, Douglas, "The Making of a Special Relationship: The United States and Israel, 1957–68," *International Journal of Middle East Studies*, Vol. 25, No. 4, November 1993, pp. 563–585.

Lons, Camille, Jonathan Fulton, Degang Sun, and Naser Al-Tamimi, *China's Great Game in the Middle East*, London: European Council on Foreign Relations, 2019. As of March 15, 2021:
https://ecfr.eu/publication/china_great_game_middle_east/

Lopez, C. Todd, *Esper: Operation Sentinel Prevents Escalation of Middle East Waterways Conflict*, Washington, D.C.: U.S. Department of Defense, July 24, 2019.

Lubold, Gordon, and Warren P. Strobel, "Biden Trimming Forces Sent to Mideast to Help Saudi Arabia," *Wall Street Journal*, April 2, 2021. As of April 6, 2021:
https://www.wsj.com/articles/biden-trimming-forces-sent-to-mideast-to-help-saudi-arabia-11617279687

Mahmoudian, Arman, and Giorgio Cafiero, "Does Russia Really Want a U.S. Return to the Iran Deal?" *IranSource*, January 19, 2021. As of March 15, 2021:
https://www.atlanticcouncil.org/blogs/iransource/does-russia-really-want-a -us-return-to-the-iran-deal/

Mann, Christopher T., *U.S. War Costs, Casualties, and Personnel Levels Since 9/11*, Washington, D.C.: Congressional Research Service, IF11182, April 18, 2019. As of March 15, 2021:
https://fas.org/sgp/crs/natsec/IF11182.pdf

Manning, Robert A., and Peter A. Wilson, "Offshore Balancing Approach Can Correct America's Middle East Approach," *The National Interest*, February 26, 2021. As of March 16, 2021:
https://nationalinterest.org/feature/offshore-balancing-strategy-can-correct -america's-middle-east-approach-178870

Mansour, Renad, Thanassis Cambanis, and Michael Wahid Hanna, "These Iraqi Militias Are Attacking Protesters and Getting Away with It. Here's Why," *Washington Post*, November 18, 2019. As of March 10, 2021:
https://www.washingtonpost.com/politics/2019/11/18/these-iraqi-militias-are -attacking-protesters-getting-away-with-it-heres-why/

Marquis, Jefferson P., Michael J. McNerney, S. Rebecca Zimmerman, Merrie Archer, Jeremy Boback, and David Stebbins, *Developing an Assessment, Monitoring, and Evaluation Framework for U.S. Department of Defense Security Cooperation*, Santa Monica, Calif.: RAND Corporation, RR-1611-AME, 2016. As of July 9, 2021:
https://www.rand.org/pubs/research_reports/RR1611.html

McDowell, Angus, "Factbox: Who's Involved in Libya's War and Why," Reuters, May 29, 2020. As of February 21, 2021:
https://www.reuters.com/article/us-libya-security-intervention-factbox/ factbox-whos-involved-in-libyas-war-and-why-idUSKBN2351W0

McGarry, Brendan W., and Emily M. Morgenstern, *Overseas Contingency Operations Funding: Background and Status*, Washington, D.C.: Congressional Research Service, R44519, September 6, 2019. As of March 15, 2021:
https://fas.org/sgp/crs/natsec/R44519.pdf

McGurk, Brett, "The Cost of an Incoherent Foreign Policy: Trump's Iran Imbroglio Undermines U.S. Priorities Everywhere Else," *Foreign Affairs*, January 22, 2020. As of February 25, 2021:
https://www.foreignaffairs.com/articles/iran/2020-01-22/cost-incoherent -foreign-policy

McVann, Christine, "Reshaping U.S. Force Posture in the Middle East," Washington, D.C.: The Washington Institute for Near East Policy, March 10, 2021. As of May 14, 2021:
https://www.washingtoninstitute.org/policy-analysis/reshaping-us-force -posture-middle-east

Mendonca, Veera, Momo Duehring, Arthur van Diesen, Jan Beise, Sinae Lee, Bin Lian, Anastasia Mshvidobadze, and Danzhen You, *MENA Generation 2030: Investing in Children and Youth Today to Secure a Prosperous Region Tomorrow*, UNICEF, Division of Data, Research, and Policy, April 2019. As of February 25, 2021:
https://data.unicef.org/resources/middle-east-north-africa-generation-2030/

Military Health System, "Traumatic Brain Injury Center of Excellence," webpage, undated. As of February 25, 2021:
https://dvbic.dcoe.mil/dod-worldwide-numbers-tbi

Miller, John W., "Biden's Mideast Drawdown Poses Perils," *Defense News*, April 15, 2021. As of May 14, 2021:
https://www.defensenews.com/opinion/commentary/2021/04/15/bidens -mideast-drawdown-poses-perils/

Moore, Elena, "Saudi Arabia and Qatar Lower Tensions in U.S.-Backed Agreement," NPR, January 5, 2021. As of May 20, 2021:
https://www.npr.org/2021/01/05/953737140/saudi-arabia-and-qatar-lower -tensions-in-us-backed-agreement

Morris, Loveday, and Hugh Naylor, "Arab States Fear Nuclear Deal Will Give Iran a Bigger Regional Role," *Washington Post*, July 14, 2015. As of February 20, 2021:
https://www.washingtonpost.com/world/middle_east/arab-states-fear -dangerous-iranian-nuclear-deal-will-shake-up-region/2015/07/14/ 96d68ff3-7fce-4bf5-9170-6bcc9dfe46aa_story.html

Mostatabi, Mana, "Sanctioning Iran's Climate," *MENASource*, May 1, 2019. As of March 15, 2021:
https://www.atlanticcouncil.org/blogs/menasource/sanctioning-iran-s -climate/

Muasher, Marwan, "Is This the Arab Spring 2.0?" Washington, D.C.: Carnegie Endowment for International Peace, October 30, 2019. As of February 25, 2021:
https://carnegieendowment.org/2019/10/30/is-this-arab-spring-2.0-pub-80220

Nadimi, Farzin, "The UN Exposes Houthi Reliance on Iranian Weapons," Washington, D.C.: The Washington Institute for Near East Policy, Policy Watch 3261, February 13, 2020. As of February 21, 2021:
https://www.washingtoninstitute.org/policy-analysis/un-exposes-houthi -reliance-iranian-weapons

Notteboom, Theo, Athanasios Pallis, and Jean-Paul Rodrigue, "Main Routing Alternatives Between East Asia and Northern Europe," *Port Economics, Management and Policy*, 2021. As of May 18, 2021: https://porteconomicsmanagement.org/pemp/contents/part1/interoceanic -passages/main-routing-alternatives-east-asia-northern-europe/

O'Donnell, Norah, "Saudi Crown Prince: If Iran Develops Nuclear Bomb, So Will We," CBS TV, March 15, 2018. As of February 20, 2021: https://www.cbsnews.com/news/saudi-crown-prince-mohammed-bin-salman -iran-nuclear-bomb-saudi-arabia/

Oehlerich, Eric, Mick Mulroy, and Liam McHugh, *Jannah or Jahannam: Options for Dealing with ISIS Detainees*, Washington, D.C.: Middle East Institute, October 2020.

Office of the Historian, "The Arab-Israeli War of 1948," webpage, undated a. As of February 21, 2021: https://history.state.gov/milestones/1945-1952/arab-israeli-war

Office of the Historian, Foreign Service Institute, "Barbary Wars, 1801–1805 and 1815–1816," webpage, undated b. As of March 15, 2021: https://history.state.gov/milestones/1801-1829/barbary-wars

Office of the Secretary of Defense, *Fiscal Year (FY) 2021 President's Budget: Justification for Security Cooperation Program and Activity Funding*, Washington D.C., April 2020.

Office of the Under Secretary of Defense, *Defense Budget Overview: United States Department of Defense Fiscal Year 2016 Budget Request*, Washington D.C., February 2015.

———, *Defense Budget Overview: United States Department of Defense Fiscal Year 2017 Budget Request*, Washington D.C., February 2016.

———, Defense Budget Overview: United States Department of Defense Fiscal Year 2018 Budget Request, Washington D.C., May 2017.

———, Defense Budget Overview: United States Department of Defense Fiscal Year 2019 Budget Request, Washington D.C., February 2018.

Oren, Michael B., *Power, Faith, and Fantasy: America in the Middle East, 1776 to the Present*, New York: W.W. Norton, 2011.

Pal, Jeremy S., and Elfatih A. B. Eltahir, "Future Temperature in Southwest Asia Projected to Exceed a Threshold for Human Adaptability," *Nature Climate Change*, Vol. 6, 2016, pp. 197–200. As of March 15, 2021: https://www.nature.com/articles/nclimate2833.pdf

Pedersen, Eric R., Kathryn E. Bouskill, Stephanie Brooks Holliday, Jonathan Cantor, Sierra Smucker, Matthew L. Mizel, Lauren Skrabala, Aaron Kofner, and Terri Tanielian, *Improving Substance Use Care: Addressing Barriers to Expanding Integrated Treatment Options for Post-9/11 Veterans*, Santa Monica, Calif.: RAND Corporation, RR-4354-WWP, 2020. As of February 25, 2021: https://www.rand.org/pubs/research_reports/RR4354.html

Peltier, Heidi, *The Cost of Debt-Financed War: Public Debt and Rising Interest for Post-9/11 War Spending*, Providence, R.I.: Brown University, Watson Institute for International & Public Affairs, January 2020. As of March 15, 2021: https://watson.brown.edu/costsofwar/files/cow/imce/papers/2020/Peltier%20 2020%20-%20The%20Cost%20of%20Debt-financed%20War.pdf

Pew Research Center, "Views of Foreign Policy," Pew Research Center, December 17, 2019. As of May 17, 2021: https://www.pewresearch.org/politics/2019/12/17/6-views-of-foreign-policy/

Priebe, Miranda, Bryan Rooney, Nathan Beauchamp-Mustafaga, Jeffrey Martini, Stephanie Pezard, *Implementing Restraint: Changes in U.S. Regional Security Policies to Operationalize a Realist Grand Strategy of Restraint*, Santa Monica, Calif.: RAND Corporation, RR-A739, 2021. As of July 9, 2021: https://www.rand.org/pubs/research_reports/RRA739-1.html

Psaledakis, Daphne, and Arshad Mohammed, "U.S. Tiptoes Through Sanctions Minefield Toward Iran Nuclear Deal," Reuters, May 17, 2021. As of May 18, 2021: https://www.reuters.com/world/middle-east/us-tiptoes-through-sanctions -minefield-toward-iran-nuclear-deal-2021-05-17/

Reagan, Ronald, "Transcript of Address by Reagan on Libya," April 15, 1986. As of May 12, 2021: https://www.nytimes.com/1986/04/15/world/transcript-of-address-by-reagan -on-libya.html

Reardon, Robert, *Containing Iran: Strategies for Addressing the Iranian Nuclear Challenge*, Santa Monica, Calif.: RAND Corporation, MG-1180-TSF, 2012. As of February 20, 2021: https://www.rand.org/pubs/monographs/MG1180.html

Regional Bureau for Arab States, *Water Governance in the Arab Region: Managing Scarcity and Securing the Future*, New York: United Nations Development Programme, 2013. As of March 15, 2021: https://www.arabstates.undp.org/content/rbas/en/home/library/huma _development/water-governance-in-the-arab-region.html

Ries, Charles, and Shelly Culbertson, "This Is How Europe Dealt with Migration," *The National Interest*, December 1, 2018. As of February 25, 2021: https://nationalinterest.org/feature/how-europe-dealt-migration-37577

Rosand, Eric, "International Efforts to Counter Violent Extremism Under President Trump: A Case Study in Dysfunction and Incoherence," Brookings, September 9, 2020. As of April 6, 2021:
https://www.brookings.edu/blog/order-from-chaos/2020/09/09/international-efforts-to-counter-violent-extremism-under-president-trump-a-case-study-in-dysfunction-and-incoherence/

Rosenblatt, Nate, *All Jihad Is Local: What ISIS' Files Tell Us About Its Fighters*, Washington, D.C.: New America, July 20, 2016.

Rubin, Alissa J., "Iraq in Worst Political Crisis in Years as Death Toll Mounts from Protests," *New York Times*, December 21, 2019. As of March 10, 2021:
https://www.nytimes.com/2019/12/21/world/middleeast/Iraq-protests-Iran.html

Rubin, Shira, "Long Sidelined, Arab Israeli Entrepreneurs Looking to Join Tech Boom with Emirati Backing," *Washington Post*, January 18, 2021. As of February 21, 2021:
https://www.washingtonpost.com/world/middle_east/israel-uae-arab-business-technology/2021/01/15/647e9efa-541a-11eb-acc5-92d2819a1ccb_story.html

Sachs, Natan, "Whose Side Are You On? Alliance Credibility in the Middle East and Japan," *Order from Chaos*, May 31, 2016. As of February 19, 2021:
https://www.brookings.edu/blog/order-from-chaos/2016/05/31/whose-side-are-you-on-alliance-credibility-in-the-middle-east-and-japan/

Savell, Stephanie, and 5W Infographics, "This Map Shows Where in the World the U.S. Military Is Combatting Terrorism," *Smithsonian Magazine*, January/February 2019. As of February 18, 2021:
https://www.smithsonianmag.com/history/map-shows-places-world-where-us-military-operates-180970997/

Schenker, David, "China and Russia: The New Threats to Middle East Security and Stability," remarks given to the Atlantic Council, Washington, D.C.: U.S. Department of State, October 8, 2019. As of March 15, 2021:
https://2017-2021.state.gov/china-and-russia-the-new-threats-to-middle-east-security-and-stability/index.html

Schroeder, Christopher M., *Startup Rising: The Entrepreneurial Revolution Remaking the Middle East*, New York: St. Martin's Press, 2013.

———, *Seeking Awesome*, newsletter, undated. As of July 10, 2021:
https://christophermschroeder.substack.com/p/coming-soon

Schwartzstein, Peter, "Climate Change and Water Woes Drove ISIS Recruiting in Iraq," *National Geographic*, November 14, 2017. As of March 15, 2021:
https://www.nationalgeographic.com/science/article/climate-change-drought-drove-isis-terrorist-recruiting-iraq

———, "The Perfect Storm: Coronavirus and Climate Change in the Middle East," Project on Middle East Democracy, April 3, 2020. As of March 15, 2021: https://pomed.org/the-perfect-storm-coronavirus-and-climate-change-in-the -middle-east/

Scobell, Andrew, and Alireza Nader, *China in the Middle East: The Wary Dragon*, Santa Monica, Calif.: RAND Corporation, RR-1229-A, 2016. As of March 15, 2021: https://www.rand.org/pubs/research_reports/RR1229.html

Sengupta, Somini, "How Biden's Climate Ambitions Could Shift America's Global Footprint," *New York Times*, January 27, 2021. As of March 9, 2021: https://www.nytimes.com/2021/01/27/us/how-bidens-climate-ambitions-could -shift-americas-global-footprint.html

Shah, Saeed, Gabriele Steinhauser, and Feliz Solomon, "Vaccine Delays in Developing Nations Risk Prolonging Pandemic," *Wall Street Journal*, February 17, 2021. As of February 25, 2021: https://www.wsj.com/articles/faltering-covid-19-vaccine-drive-in-developing -world-risks-prolonging-pandemic-11613557801

Shaikh, Shaan, "Missiles and Rockets of Hezbollah," Missile Threat, Center for Strategic and International Studies, June 26, 2018 (last modified September 27, 2019). As of February 21, 2021: https://missilethreat.csis.org/country/hezbollahs-rocket-arsenal

Sharp, Jeremy M., Christopher M. Blanchard, and Sarah R. Collins, *Congress and the War in Yemen: Oversight and Legislation 2015–2020*, Washington, D.C.: Congressional Research Service, R45046, June 19, 2020.

Sharp, Jeremy M., Jim Zanotti, Kenneth Katzman, Christina L. Arabia, and Clayton Thomas, *Israel's Qualitative Military Edge and Possible U.S. Arms Sales to the United Arab Emirates*, Washington, D.C.: Congressional Research Service, R46580, October 26, 2020. As of March 15, 2021: https://crsreports.congress.gov/product/pdf/R/R46580

Simon, Steven, and Richard Sokolsky, "What to Do With U.S. Forces in the Persian Gulf," *Foreign Policy*, April 16, 2021. As of May 14, 2021: https://foreignpolicy.com/2021/04/16/troops-afghanistan-persian-gulf -withdrawal-biden/

Singerman, Diane, *The Economic Imperatives of Marriage: Emerging Practices and Identities Among Youth in the Middle East*, Dubai, UAE: Wolfensohn Center for Development, Dubai School of Government, Middle East Youth Initiative Working Paper No. 6, September 2007.

Singh, Michael, *China and the United States in the Middle East: Between Dependency and Rivalry*, Washington, D.C.: Washington Institute for Near East Policy, September 2020a. As of March 15, 2021:
https://www.washingtoninstitute.org/policy-analysis/china-and-united-states
-middle-east-between-dependency-and-rivalry

———, *U.S. Policy in the Middle East amid Great Power Competition*, Beaver Creek, Colo.: Reagan Institute Strategy Group, 2020b. As of March 15, 2021:
https://www.washingtoninstitute.org/policy-analysis/us-policy-middle-east
-amid-great-power-competition

Sladden, James, Becca Wasser, Ben Connable, and Sarah Grand-Clement, *Russian Strategy in the Middle East*, Santa Monica, Calif.: RAND Corporation, PE-236-RC, 2017. As of February 19, 2021:
https://www.rand.org/pubs/perspectives/PE236.html

Smeltz, Dina, and Craig Kafura, *American Public Support for U.S. Troops in Middle East Has Grown*, Chicago, Ill.: The Chicago Council on Global Affairs, February 10, 2020. As of March 15, 2021:
https://www.thechicagocouncil.org/research/public-opinion-survey/american
-public-support-us-troops-middle-east-has-grown

Soliman, Mohammed, "The GCC, US-China Tech War, and the Next 5G Storm," Washington, D.C.: The Middle East Institute, September 1, 2020. As of March 15, 2021:
https://www.mei.edu/publications/gcc-us-china-tech-war-and-next-5g-storm

Spacapan, John, "Conventional Wisdom Says That Turkey Won't Go Nuclear. That Might Be Wrong," *Bulletin of the Atomic Scientists*, July 7, 2020. As of February 20, 2021:
https://thebulletin.org/2020/07/conventional-wisdom-says-turkey-wont-go
-nuclear-that-might-be-wrong/

The State Council, The People's Republic of China, "Full Text of China's Arab Policy Paper," webpage, January 13, 2016. As of March 15, 2021:
http://english.www.gov.cn/archive/publications/2016/01/13/content
_281475271412746.htm

———, "Full Text: China and the World in the New Era," webpage, September 27, 2019. As of March 15, 2021:
http://english.www.gov.cn/archive/whitepaper/201909/27/content_WS5d8d80
f9c6d0bcf8c4c142ef.html

Strobel, Warren P., "Biden Launches Fresh Effort to End Civil War in Yemen, Halting 'Offensive' Aid to Saudis, Naming Envoy," *Wall Street Journal*, February 4, 2021. As of February 19, 2021:
https://www.wsj.com/articles/biden-to-name-special-envoy-to-yemen-launching
-fresh-effort-to-end-the-fighting-11612450815

Sude, Barbara, David Stebbins, and Sarah Weilant, *Lessening the Risk of Refugee Radicalization: Lessons for the Middle East from Past Crises*, Santa Monica, Calif.: RAND Corporation, PE-166-OSD, 2015. As of February 25, 2021:
https://www.rand.org/pubs/perspectives/PE166.html

Sullivan, Gregory, Audit Director, "Operation Inherent Resolve—Summary of Work Performed by the Department of the Treasury Related to Terrorist Financing, ISIS, and Anti-Money Laundering for First Quarter Fiscal Year 2021," memorandum to Department of Defense Lead Inspector General, Washington, D.C., January 4, 2021. As of February 25, 2021:
https://oig.treasury.gov/sites/oig/files/2021-01/OIG-CA-21-012.pdf

Tabatabai, Ariane M., and Becca Wasser, "Could America Use Its Leverage to Alter the Saudis' Behavior?" *Newsweek*, November 15, 2018. As of February 19, 2021:
https://www.newsweek.com/saudi-arabia-needs-america-now-may-be-time
-trump-use-leverage-1217864

Thomas, Clayton, Jeremy Sharp, Christopher M. Blanchard, and Christina L. Arabia, *Arms Sales in the Middle East: Trends and Analytical Perspectives for U.S. Policy*, Washington, D.C.: Congressional Research Service, November 23, 2020. As of March 15, 2021:
https://fas.org/sgp/crs/mideast/R44984.pdf

Tol, Gönül, and Ömer Taşpınar, "Turkey's Russian Roulette," in Karim Mezran and Arturo Varvelli, eds., *The MENA Region: A Great Power Competition*, Milan: ISPI and Atlantic Council, 2019, pp. 107–125.

"Top Iran General Says Destroying Israel 'Achievable Goal,'" *VOA News*, September 30, 2019. As of February 20, 2021:
https://www.voanews.com/middle-east/top-iran-general-says-destroying
-israel-achievable-goal

Transparency International, "What People Think: Corruption in the Middle East and North Africa," December 11, 2019. As of March 4, 2021:
https://www.transparency.org/en/news/what-people-think-corruption-in
-the-middle-east-north-africa

UNHCR—*See* United Nations High Commissioner for Refugees.

UNICEF—*See* United Nations Children's Fund.

United Nations, "Peace Agreements Database Search: Israel," 2019. As of February 21, 2021:
https://peacemaker.un.org/document-search

United Nations, *UN Comtrade Database*, Online Database, Department of Economic and Social Affairs, Statistics Division, Trade Statistics, March 15, 2021. As of March 15, 2021:
https://comtrade.un.org/

United Nations Children's Fund, Middle East and North Africa, "Education Response to COVID-19," webpage, undated. As of February 25, 2021: https://www.unicef.org/mena/education

United Nations High Commissioner for Refugees, *Global Trends: Forced Displacement in 2019*, Copenhagen, Denmark, June 18, 2020. As of February 25, 2021: https://www.unhcr.org/5ee200e37.pdf

———, "Government Partners," webpage, undated a. As of February 25, 2021: https://www.unhcr.org/en-us/donors.html

———, "Resettlement Data Finder (RDF)," webpage, undated b. As of February 25, 2021: https://rsq.unhcr.org/en/#j4VK

Urdal, Henrik, "A Clash of Generations? Youth Bulges and Political Violence," *International Studies Quarterly*, Vol. 50, 2006, pp. 607–629.

U.S. Agency for International Development, *Foreign Aid Explorer*, Online Database, USAID Data Services. As of March 24, 2021: https://explorer.usaid.gov/data

U.S. Department of Commerce, Office of Trade Agreements Negotiation and Compliance, "Bilateral Investment Treaties," webpage, undated. As of February 18, 2021: https://tcc.export.gov/Trade_Agreements/Bilateral_Investment_Treaties/index.asp

U.S. Department of Defense, *Quadrennial Defense Review Report*, Washington, D.C., February 2010. As of March 15, 2021: https://archive.defense.gov/qdr/QDR%20as%20of%2029JAN10%201600.pdf

———, "Separate U.S. Airstrikes Kill 2 Senior al-Qaida Leaders in Syria," *DOD News*, January 17, 2017. As of May 18, 2021: https://www.defense.gov/Explore/News/Article/Article/1054426/separate-us-airstrikes-kill-2-senior-al-qaida-leaders-in-syria/

———, *Summary of the 2018 National Defense Strategy of the United States of America: Sharpening the American Military's Competitive Edge*, Washington, D.C., January 20, 2018. As of March 10, 2021: https://dod.defense.gov/Portals/1/Documents/pubs/2018-National-Defense-Strategy-Summary.pdf

U.S. Department of State, "U.S. Relations with Saudi Arabia," Bilateral Relations Fact Sheet, Washington, D.C.: Bureau of Near Eastern Affairs, December 15, 2020. As of May 18, 2021: https://www.state.gov/u-s-relations-with-saudi-arabia/

———, "U.S. Relations with Yemen," Bilateral Relations Fact Sheet, Washington, D.C.: Bureau of Near Eastern Affairs, December 30, 2020. As of February 19, 2021:
https://www.state.gov/u-s-relations-with-yemen/

———, "Major Non-NATO Ally Status," Fact Sheet, Washington, D.C.: Bureau of Political-Military Affairs, January 20, 2021. As of February 18, 2021:
https://www.state.gov/major-non-nato-ally-status/

———, "Joint Statement by the Secretary of State of the United States of America and the Foreign Ministers of France, Germany, and the United Kingdom," Media Note, Washington, D.C.: Office of the Spokesperson, February 18, 2021. As of February 20, 2021:
https://www.state.gov/joint-statement-by-the-secretary-of-state-of-the-united
-states-of-america-and-the-foreign-ministers-of-france-germany-the-united
-kingdom/

U.S. Department of State, "Major Non-NATO Ally Status," Fact Sheet, Washington, D.C.: Bureau of Political-Military Affairs, January 20, 2021.

———, "The Abraham Accords," webpage, undated. As of February 21, 2021:
https://www.state.gov/the-abraham-accords/

U.S. Energy Information Administration, *International Energy Outlook 2019*, Washington, D.C., September 24, 2019. As of May 18, 2021:
https://www.eia.gov/outlooks/archive/ieo19/

———, "U.S. Total Crude Oil and Products Imports," Excel file, January 29, 2021b. As of February 10, 2021:
https://www.eia.gov/dnav/pet/pet_move_impcus_a2_nus_ep00_im0_mbblpd
_a.htm

———, "Total Crude Oil and Products Exports by Destination," Excel file, January 29, 2021c.

U.S. Institute of Peace, "Biden & Iran: The Nuclear Deal," *The Iran Primer*, updated March 9, 2021. As of March 11, 2021:
https://iranprimer.usip.org/blog/2021/jan/13/biden-iran-nuclear-deal

U.S. Trade Representative, "Free Trade Agreements," webpage, undated a. As of February 18, 2021:
https://ustr.gov/trade-agreements/free-trade-agreements

———, "Trade and Investment Framework Agreements," webpage, undated c. As of February 18, 2021:
https://ustr.gov/trade-agreements/trade-investment-framework-agreements

Vahdat, Amir, and Jon Gambrell, "Iran Leader Says Israel a 'Cancerous Tumor' to Be Destroyed," AP News, May 22, 2020. As of February 20, 2021:
https://apnews.com/article/a033042303545d9ef783a95222d51b83

Walker, Hunter, "Jimmy Carter: 'I Could Have Wiped Iran off the Map,'" *Business Insider*, October 1, 2014. As of February 25, 2021:
https://www.businessinsider.com/jimmy-carter-i-could-have-wiped-iran-off
-the-map-2014-10

Wallin, Matthew, *U.S. Military Bases and Facilities in the Middle East*, Fact Sheet, American Security Project, June 2018.

Watson Institute for International and Public Affairs, "Costs of War: Summary of Findings," webpage, undated a. As of February 25, 2021:
https://watson.brown.edu/costsofwar/papers/summary

———, "Costs of War: U.S. & Allied Killed," webpage, undated b. As of February 25, 2021:
https://watson.brown.edu/costsofwar/costs/human/military/killed

Wechsler, William F., "U.S. Withdrawal from the Middle East: Perceptions and Reality," in Karim Mezran and Arturo Varvelli, eds., *The MENA Region: A Great Power Competition*, Milan: ISPI and the Atlantic Council, 2019, pp. 13–38. As of March 15, 2021:
https://www.ispionline.it/sites/default/files/pubblicazioni/ispi_report_mena
_region_2019.pdf

Wehrey, Frederic, Michele Dunne, Robert Springborg, Emile Hokayem, Becca Wasser, Jodi Vittori, Jonathan D. Caverley, Hassan Maged, Jalel Harchaoui, Andrew S. Weiss, Patricia M. Kim, "From Hardware to Holism: Rebalancing America's Security Engagement with Arab States," Washington, D.C.: Carnegie Endowment for International Peace, May 18, 2021. As of May 18, 2021:
https://carnegieendowment.org/2021/05/18/from-hardware-to-holism-rebalancing
-america-s-security-engagement-with-arab-states-pub-84520

Weinthal, Erika, and Neda Zawahri, "Don't Politicize Water," *Foreign Policy*, September 17, 2020. As of March 15, 2021:
https://foreignpolicy.com/2020/09/17/water-cooperation-middle-east/

Werrell, Caitlin E., and Fancesco Femia, "Fragile States: The Nexus of Climate Change, State Fragility and Migration," *ANGLE Journal*, November 24, 2015. As of March 15, 2021:
https://anglejournal.com/article/2015-11-fragile-states-the-nexus-of-climate
-change-state-fragility-and-migration/

Wezeman, Pieter D., Aude Fleurant, Alexandra Kuimova, Diego Lopes da Silva, Nan Tian, and Siemon T. Wezeman, "Trends in International Arms Transfers, 2019," SIPRI Fact Sheet, Stockholm: Stockholm International Peace Research Institute, March 2020. As of March 15, 2021:
https://www.sipri.org/sites/default/files/2020-03/fs_2003_at_2019.pdf

The White House, "Statement by the President," August 7, 2014. As of April 6, 2021:
https://obamawhitehouse.archives.gov/the-press-office/2014/08/07/statement-president

———, *National Security Strategy of the United States of America*, Washington, D.C., December 2017.

———, "Statement from the Press Secretary Regarding the Designations of the UAE and Kingdom of Bahrain as Major Security Partners of the United States," Washington, D.C., January 15, 2021a. As of February 18, 2021:
https://trumpwhitehouse.archives.gov/briefings-statements/statement-press-secretary-regarding-designations-uae-kingdom-bahrain-major-strategic-partners-united-states/

———, "Remarks by President Biden on America's Place in the World," Washington, D.C., February 4, 2021b. As of February 19, 2021:
https://www.whitehouse.gov/briefing-room/speeches-remarks/2021/02/04/remarks-by-president-biden-on-americas-place-in-the-world/

———, *Interim National Security Strategic Guidance*, Washington, D.C., March 2021c. As of March 10, 2021:
https://www.whitehouse.gov/wp-content/uploads/2021/03/NSC-1v2.pdf

Winter, Charlie, Shiraz Maher, and Aymenn Jawad al-Tamimi, *Understand Salafi-Jihadist Attitudes Towards Innovation*, London: International Centre for the Study of Radicalisation, 2021.

World Bank, "GDP Growth (Annual %)–Middle East & North Africa," webpage, undated a. As of March 12, 2021:
https://data.worldbank.org/indicator/NY.GDP.MKTP.KD.ZG?locations=ZQ

———, "Population, Total—Middle East & North Africa," webpage, undated c. As of February 25, 2021:
https://data.worldbank.org/indicator/SP.POP.TOTL?locations=ZQ

Wormuth, Christine, *Russia and China in the Middle East: Implications for the United States in an Era of Strategic Competition*, testimony presented before the House Foreign Affairs Subcommittee on Middle East, North Africa and International Terrorism on May 9, 2019, Santa Monica, Calif.: RAND Corporation, CT-511, 2019. As of February 25, 2021:
https://www.rand.org/pubs/testimonies/CT511.html

Wyne, Ali, and Colin P. Clarke, "Assessing China and Russia's Moves in the Middle East," *Lawfare*, September 17, 2020. As of March 15, 2021:
https://www.lawfareblog.com/assessing-china-and-russias-moves-middle-east

Zelin, Aaron Y., *Wilayat al-Hawl: 'Remaining' and Incubating the Next Islamic State Generation*, Washington, D.C.: Washington Institute for Near East Policy, October 18, 2019.

Zelin, Aaron, and Michael Knights, *The Islamic State's Resurgence in the COVID Era? From Defeat to Renewal in Iraq and Syria*, Washington, D.C.: Washington Institute for Near East Policy, May 29, 2020.